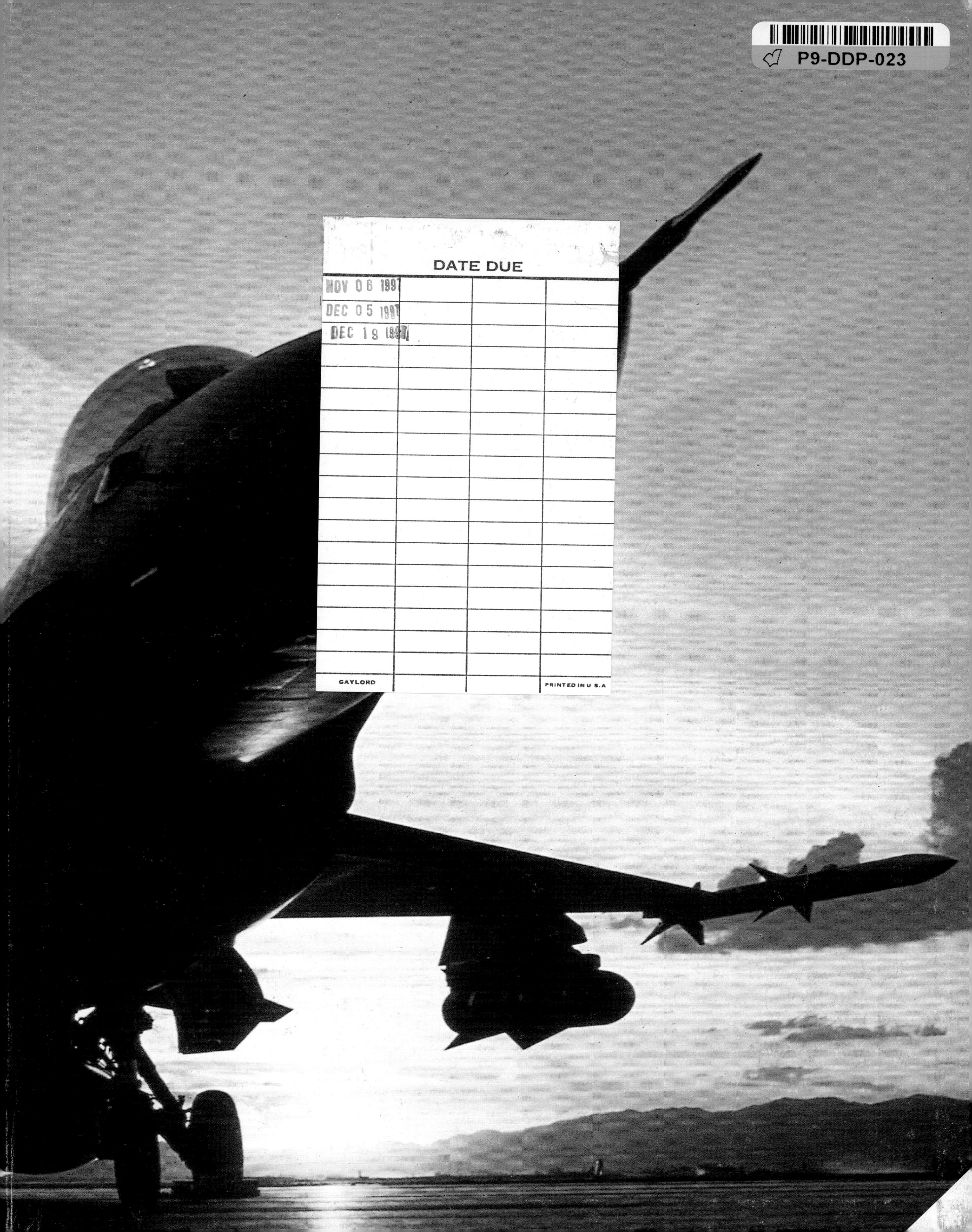

COMBAT AIRCRAFT

F-16

CRESCENT BOOKS
New York

A Salamander Book

This edition © Salamander Books Ltd, 1992

This 1992 edition published by
Crescent Books
distributed by Outlet Book Company, Inc,
A Random House Company,
225 Park Avenue South,
New York, New York 10003.

Printed and Bound in Hong Kong

ISBN 0 517 06737 4

8 7 6 5 4 3 2 1

Credits

Project Manager: Ray Bonds

Editors: Bernard Fitzsimons, Tony Hall

Designer: Rod Teasdale. This edition
adapted by Studio Gossett

Diagrams: TIGA
(© Salamander Books Ltd.)

**Three-views, cutaway drawing and color
profiles**: © Pilot Press Ltd.

Scrap line drawings: Mike Badrocke
(© Salamander Books Ltd.)

Jacket: Kai Choi

Contents

Acknowledgements

This book would not have been possible
without the unstinting help over the
years of current and former members of
the public relations department at the
Fort Worth Division of General
Dynamics, and of technicians on the
assembly and flight lines. Many other
companies have provided material:
apart from those credited for supplying
photographs, these include Itek, Martin
Marietta, McDonnell Douglas, and
Oldelft. Thanks are also due to many
departments and units of the USAF, to
the air arms of Belgium, Denmark, the
Netherlands and Norway, and to their
military attaches in London, and to the
Editor and Defence Editor of *Flight
International* for research facilities.

Authors

Doug Richardson is a defence journalist
specializing in the fields of aviation,
guided missiles and electronics. Editor
of *Defence Materiel*, the journal
devoted to the British defence industry,
he trained initially as an electronics
engineer, starting his career as a
technician with an R&D team working
on avionics for the Buccaneer and the
cancelled TSR-2 project.

After an electronics R&D career
encompassing such diverse areas as
radar, electronic warfare, rocket engine
control systems, computers, automatic
test equipment and missile trials, he
switched to technical journalism as a
member of the staff of the internationally
respected aerospace journal *Flight
International*, serving as Defence Editor
before moving on to become Editor of
the international technical defence
journal *Military Technology and
Economics*.

His previous work for Salamander
includes *The Illustrated Encyclopedia
of Modern Warplanes*, *Weapons of the
Gulf War*, and contributions to *The
Balance of Military Power*. He has also
written for such technical and defence
journals as *International Defense
Review*, *NATO's 15 Nations*, *Defence*,
Technologia Militar and *Wehrtechnik*.

Filmset by Tradespools Ltd. This edition set and adapted by SX Composing Ltd.

Color reproduction by Rodney Howe Ltd., Scantrans PTE Ltd., Singapore

Introduction

General Dynamics' Fighting Falcon was one of the stars of the 1977 Paris Air Show. In those not-so-distant days it was simply designated F-16 and only a handful of aircraft were flying, but the type was regarded by many observers as the hottest and probably the most controversial fighter in the Western world.

As the aircraft stood on display in the flight line, many individuals stopped to photograph it, but one in particular caught the writer's eye. Dressed in a suit of distinctly out-of-date style and equipped with a Russian camera fitted with a large telephoto lens, he was photographing the aircraft not from close up but from a range of several hundred yards.

The resulting clandestine photographs were no doubt eagerly examined in an East European Defence Ministry a few days later, but the whole exercise might have been made easier had the anonymous photographer simply marched boldly up to the F-16 and accepted one of the colour photos of the aircraft which the two GD men on duty beside it were

handing out to anyone who asked!

At a time when most of the Western European media saw the F-16 as a potential political scandal, and news reports knocking the aircraft were commonplace, the Warsaw Pact was clearly taking the new GD warplane very seriously – even if one of their intelligence-gathering methods was a trifle crude.

Subsequent events can have done little to allay their concern. Far from being the 'can of worms' which its opponents had suggested, Fighting Falcon is a highly capable aircraft which has successfully met the needs of air forces in five of the seven continents.

To date, the only "Super-F-16" likely to leave the drawing board is Japan's canard-equipped SX-3. Back at Fort Worth, however, the design team is already drawing up plans for new fighters to meet the USAF's Multi-Role Fighter requirement.

Development

No other combat aircraft has packed as much multirole military capability into a single airframe as does the F-16 Fighting Falcon. Agile enough to outfly opponents such as third-generation MiG-21s, yet able to carry heavy ordnance loads over long ranges during strike missions, the F-16 will form a major component of Western air strength during the 1980s and 1990s. For the first time in modern fighter design 'lightweight' is not a euphemism for 'limited performance', and Fighting Falcon is a triumph for the advocates of smaller, lighter and less expensive fighters.

In following up the F-86 Sabre of the late 1940s, US fighter designers developed an expensive fascination with the sophistication made possible by improvements in technology. The larger the aircraft, the more capable it became, but while succeeding designs saw massive increases in combat capability, the price was paid in terms of both money and ever-diminishing fleet numbers. From the P-51 Mustang to the F-15 Eagle, each new US land-based fighter was on average 2·4 times more expensive than its predecessor, and Eagle production over 15 years may never reach a tenth of the 15,000 Mustangs built in a third of that time.

This philosophy was challenged briefly in the light of Korean War experience. The F-104 should have ended up a US equivalent of the MiG-21 Fishbed, but like the earlier F-100 evolved into a strike fighter instead of an air-combat fighter. Early models were used in Vietnam for a short time, but the USAF found itself having to combat the agile and lightweight MiGs of the North Vietnamese air force with the heavy and expensive F-4 Phantom – a type originally developed as an all-weather naval interceptor. The subsequent addi-

tion of wing slats and a built-in 20mm cannon enhanced the aircraft's usefulness as an air combat fighter, and the F-4E was to have a long and successful combat career, but the original design had never been intended for dogfighting.

The Vietnam experience

Over North Vietnam, the US pilots found themselves unable to match the kill rates of the Korean War. Instead of a 10:1 or better kill ratio of the earlier conflict, they achieved at best just over 3:1, a figure which steadily fell to still lower values. For a long time, the US services claimed to have maintained permanent superiority over the MiGs, quoting rates of just over unity at worst. In practice, the ratio at times came out slightly in favour of the Vietnamese.

Part of the problem was training programmes which had placed little emphasis on air-to-air combat. The accepted dogma was that the traditional dogfight had a hallowed place in the history of air fighting, but none at all in modern warfare. Even in the early 1940s, the Spitfires and Hurricanes used to defend British skies from the attentions of the Luftwaffe were committed to combat using elaborate pre-planned

tactics which virtually denied the possibility of individual 'free-style' air-to-air engagements. The Luftwaffe pilots had no such illusions, and took a heavy toll of the defenders in early encounters.

With the arrival of the high-speed jet fighter, and the subsequent development of supersonic fighters, the 'no-dogfighting' dogma re-emerged virtually unchanged from its early 1940s RAF form. In view of the speed of the latest warplanes, the firing time available to an attacker was thought to be so small that pilots attempting to dogfight would have little chance of hitting their targets. Long-range combat using air-to-air missiles was thought to be the likely pattern of future combat. In the skies above Korea, Suez, and the Indo-Pakistan border the falsehood of this theory has been demonstrated time and again. In the light of the Vietnam experience it was rejected by the USAF.

As early as 1965 the USAF began concept-formulation studies of new high-performance fighters. These included a heavy 60,000lb (27,000kg) interceptor/air-superiority fighter designated Fighter Experimental (FX), and a lightweight Advanced Day Fighter (ADF). FX would have been heavier

than the F-4 Phantom, with twin engines and a variable-geometry wing, while the 25,000lb (11,000kg) ADF design specified a thrust-to-weight ratio and wing loading intended to better the performance of the MiG-21 by a margin of 25 per cent.

The appearance of the Soviet MiG-25 Foxbat fighter in the mid-1960s created a hiatus in USAF future fighter plans. Foxbat posed the threat of the Soviet air force and its Warsaw Pact allies being equipped with Mach 3 fighters at a time when the USAF had only a handful of experimental Mach 3 YF-12 fighter prototypes and no plans for production of aircraft in this performance class. Development of the massive North American F-108 Rapier interceptor had begun in the late 1950s, but this Mach 3 design

Above: Contrasting styles in fighter design – 15 years separated the first flights of the F-4 Phantom (left) and the YF-16 (right).

Below: Dogfighters old and new in formation provide graphic evidence that Fighting Falcon is hardly bigger than the 1940s P-51 Mustang. Note the 'bubble' canopies.

was cancelled in September 1959, 18 months before the first of two prototypes was due to fly.

Foxbat's Mach 3 capability provoked a redirection of USAF fighter planning. The urgent goal now was to develop a design capable of matching both the existing MiG-21 and the new MiG-25, shifting the emphasis to an FX design – the F-15 – offering a high top speed and long-range missile armament.

Although on 'back-burner', the concept of a lightweight fighter similar to ADF was not dead. Two individuals who did much to keep the concept of a lightweight fighter alive were former fighter instructor Major John Boyd, and Pierre Sprey, a civilian working for the assistant Secretary of Defense for Systems Analysis.

Boyd had already had a strong influence on the FX project and was the inventor of the concept of energy manoeuvrability – a vital element in assessing fighter performance. "Let's pretend that manoeuvrability is an energy problem", he once suggested to a group of thermodynamics students. "When you manoeuvre an airplane you need energy ... you lose energy either in gaining altitude, airspeed or both.

"Normally you lose energy in turning. What happens is that your drag exceeds your thrust, and at that point you have a negative energy rate. That negative rate has to come out of altitude, airspeed or out of a combination of the two. You reach a point, even with your military afterburner, at which drag is greater than thrust. That means you have a negative vector ... you multiply net drag by velocity and that tells you how much energy you're going to have to pump up."

Measuring performance

At first Boyd could hardly believe that this simple idea was a new method of looking at fighter performance. Once he had accepted the fact, he considered how combinations of aerodynamics and engines could be devised to create better aircraft. "You just turn the problem of manoeuvrability around and look at it from a different viewpoint. And the result of that was obvious.... The right thrust-to-weight ratio would give you an important edge over your adversary." Fighter performance could be measured at different combinations of altitude, airspeed and manoeuvring situations in terms of what is now designated Specific Excess Power – Ps in engineering jargon.

Boyd's theory showed that the FX would require an engine with a thrust-to-weight ratio significantly better than that of current designs. The resulting F100 turbofan was not only used to power the F-15, but also created the possibility of a lightweight single-engined design of high performance.

Traditional USAF thinking prior to the

early 1970s equated light weight with short range. To some degree, this was justified in view of the technology of the time. The MiG-21 was a lightweight developed using mid-1950s technology, and the original Fishbed C day fighter gave rise to the quip among export users that it was a 'supersonic sports plane' – an aircraft with very limited range and even more limited payload.

In the late 1960s, Boyd and Sprey devised a 25,000lb (11,340kg) design designated F-XX – a dedicated air superiority fighter of high endurance. Later studies took this weight down even lower to around 17,000lb (7,700kg). The concept met much opposition, since some saw it as a threat both to traditional thinking on the subject of fighters and to the existing F-15 project.

By 1971, Boyd was working for the Air Force Prototype Study Group. Conse-

quently, he was able to push the concept at a time when the idea of competitive flight-testing of prototype designs was returning to vogue after the massive and highly controversial Total Procurement Package contracts of the 1960s which had resulted in the F-111 and C-5 Galaxy.

Main driving force in getting the LWF project off the drawing board and into the experimental shop was Deputy Defense Secretary David A. Packard, who saw the concept of competitive prototyping as a method of reversing the ever-growing cost of new weapon systems. A series of ground rules for such prototyping exercises drawn up by Air Force Secretary Robert C. Seamans specified that funding would be limited, with initial performance goals and military specifications kept to a minimum. Contestants should not be constrained by

Above: The Convair F-106 was built only in small numbers, but the YF-16 from the same Fort Worth plant was the first of at least 2,000.

the existing force structure of the USAF, but should not assume that any long-term production commitment existed.

Two USAF requirements were chosen for prototyping: a medium STOL transport intended to replace the C-130 Hercules, and the lightweight fighter. These resulted in the Boeing YC-14 and McDonnell Douglas YC-15 jet transports and the YF-16 and YF-17 fighter prototypes. Instead of the 'XC-' and 'XF-' designations which would have been traditional for such programmes, the 'Y' (development) prefix was used in order to stress that a mixture of off-the-shelf and experimental technologies were being used.

The first YF-16, serial 72-1567 was rolled out at Fort Worth in December 1973, only 21 months after contract award. Following an 'unofficial' and unplanned first flight on January 20, 1974, it was used to clear the flight envelope, achieving supersonic speed on its third official sortie. Along with the second prototype it took part in the fly-off against the Northrop YF-17, and was flown against MiG-17 and MiG-21 fighters.

Above: The YF-16s did much experimental work with ordnance and missiles. Here the second aircraft carries Paveway laser-guided bombs on underwing pylons and an Atlis laser designator under the intake.

Above right: Definitive F-16 configuration with the enlarged tail.

Above: When first rolled out the second YF-16 was painted in a blue-on-white camouflage scheme devised **by GD. It was later repainted in red, white and blue to match the first aircraft, then in all grey.**

Four contracts worth a total of around $100 million were placed early in 1972 under the LWF programme. General Dynamics was given $38 million to develop and fly two YF-16s, while Northrop was awarded $39 million for two prototypes of the rival YF-17. Contracts were also given to Pratt & Whitney for development of a version of the F100 turbofan specifically for single-engined installations, and to General Electric for the new and smaller YF101 engine.

In submitting a Request for Proposals (RFP) for what was now designated the Lightweight Fighter (LWF) to industry in early 1972, the USAF specified three main objectives. The resulting design should fully explore the advantages of emerging technologies, reduce the risk and uncertainties involved in full-scale development and production of a new fighter, and provide the Department of Defense with a variety of technological options available to meet military hardware needs.

Instead of trying to match the 'brochure' capability of Soviet fighters, the USAF decided to optimize the LWF for the likely conditions of future air combat – altitudes of 30,000 to 40,000ft (9,000 to 12,000m) and speeds of Mach 0.6 to 1.6 – with no attempt to equal the performance of the MiG-25 Foxbat. It was designed not for the top right-hand corner of the performance envelope, but for a wide range of flight conditions, and with the emphasis on turn rate, acceleration and range. This combination of parameters would allow the resulting aircraft to intercept and engage not only existing Warsaw Pact types such as the MiG-21, MiG-23 and Su-7, but also more advanced aircraft such as developed MiG-23 versions and the Su-24 Fencer.

The choice of likely operating height would raise a few eyebrows today, when most combat aircraft must fly at treetop height in order to survive, but reflects a time before the surface-to-air missile threat had literally brought the USAF down to earth. Even in the mid-1970s, the concept of flying into hostile airspace at medium altitude under the cover of advanced ECM had still not been abandoned.

Prototype technology
Following industrial submissions by five companies, General Dynamics and Northrop were chosen to develop flight-test hardware, and a contract was awarded to General Dynamics on April 13, 1972. This was a 'cost plus fixed fee' contract worth $37·9 million, and covered the design, construction and test of two prototypes under the USAF designation YF-16, plus one year of flight testing.

Although development and testing of these light fighters was a technology-demonstration programme, the USAF retained the option of carrying on to develop the design into a service aircraft. The contract with GD specified an average flyaway unit cost target of $3.0 million in 1972 dollars, (rather more in 1983 prices), assuming a production run of 300 examples at a rate of 100 per year. Complete design responsibility for the aircraft lay with the contractors, in order to reduce paperwork and maintain the pace of the programme, under the direction of the Aeronautical Systems Division at Wright-Patterson AFB, which monitored both projects throughout subsequent development.

No attempt was made in designing the YF-16 to push individual technological advances: the intention was to produce and test an aircraft capable of being developed into an operational type. New technology was used in in-

Above: According to some critics, the F-16 should have retained the YF-16 configuration shown here – a simple day fighter armed with two AIM-9, a cannon and minimal avionics.

stances where it would have the greatest effect in meeting performance targets, but proven systems and components were retained in areas where such new technology was not required. Components and detail assemblies were designed for ease of manufacture, using low-cost materials wherever possible. Hardware was standardized wherever possible, the design of the air-

Below: In creating the full-scale development F-16s GD engineers increased the areas of the wing, horizontal stabilizers and ventral strakes and re-configured the forward fuselage to accommodate a nose radar. The third FSD aircraft, 75- **0747, flew for the first time on May 3, 1977, and was the first to be fitted with the full avionics and fire-control system. This aircraft was the only F-16 to carry the two-tone dark grey-on-grey camouflage scheme.**

USAF 50747

AF
01 568

frame often incorporating multi-use parts and assemblies.

Flying advanced technology features on the YF-16 gave the USAF confidence to adopt them in a service aircraft. "If we hadn't put them in the prototype, we'd still be arguing about putting them into a production airplane", F-16 director of engineering Willian C. Dietz told the US magazine *Aviation Week & Space Technology* in 1977. Although high-technology features such as relaxed stability, fly-by-wire control, wing/body blending and strakes, variable camber and the reclining seat were used to improve F-16 performance, these were not seen as high risks in terms of production or maintenance.

Specific cost goals were set at an early stage, and careful studies were carried out to establish areas where a trade-off between cost and performance or operational capability would be acceptable.

Prototype design
Design objective of the YF-16 was to create the maximum agility and manoeuvrability in a small aircraft with minimum avionics capable of conducting air combat operations some 500nm (575 miles/926km) from its own base.

Small size not only dictated design simplicity, but brought a series of other advantages. Factors such as material, detail design and construction being equal, airframe cost is largely dependent on airframe weight, so the move towards a smaller aircraft promised lower costs. At the same time, drag was minimized, allowing a lower thrust setting to be used during aircraft cruise, and increasing the thrust-to-weight ratio possible with any given powerplant. And as experience in Vietnam had shown, the small size of the MiG-17 and MiG-21 made them difficult to detect visually, adding to the problems of aircrew engaging these types in air combat.

One factor which helped focus USAF attention on the virtues of the YF-16 and YF-17 was the Middle East War of 1973. The USAF has always fought its wars under conditions of numerical superiority, but October of that year saw a close ally struggling to win air and battlefield superiority against forces abundantly

equipped along Soviet lines. The need of quantity as well as quality was brought home in a conflict in which one observer estimates that some 40 per cent of the Israeli fighter force was lost, or damaged to the point where it was not available for combat, within the first two days.

One influence on the size of the design was the likely avionics payload. While the LWF requirement specified minimal avionics, the design team recognized that an operational aircraft would probably require a heavier and bulkier payload of electronics. Accordingly, the decision was made not to size the basic aircraft to handle radar-guided missiles such as the AIM-7 Sparrow, but to assume an air-to-air armament of heat-seeking AIM-9 Sidewinder missiles plus a General Electric M61 cannon, while making provisions within

the design to allow Sparrow-class missiles to be incorporated at a later date, should this be desired.

Military requirements specified a load factor of 7·33g while carrying 80 per cent internal fuel. GD decided to increase this figure to 9·0g at full internal fuel, and to increase the service life of the airframe from the normal 4,000 hours to 8,000 hours.

Accepting the fact that fighters invariably end up carrying external fuel tanks, the GD team decided to capitalize on this trend. Assuming that a YF-16 pilot would use externally-carried fuel on the outbound trip to the combat zone, then fight and return on internal fuel, the design team allocated internal fuel volume accordingly, reducing the airframe size. This move shaved 1,470lb (667kg) off the airframe empty weight, and reduced all-up weight by

Above: This head-on view of a YF-16 shows the wing leading-edge strakes and the way the wing is blended smoothly into the fuselage.

3,300lb (1497kg). More importantly, turn rate could as a result be increased by five per cent, and acceleration by 30 per cent.

Before deciding on a configuration for the new aircraft, GD engineers considered the effect of 78 variables, running theoretical analyses and wind-tunnel tests. The latter testing totalled 1,272 hours, and was carried out at speeds from Mach 0·2 up to Mach 2·2, at angles of attack of up to 28deg and at yaw angles of up to 12deg. Parameters identified as having a significant influence on performance included wing sweep, camber and aerofoil section, inlet position and shape, the incorpora-

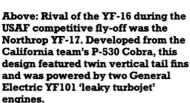

Above: Rival of the YF-16 during the USAF competitive fly-off was the Northrop YF-17. Developed from the California team's P-530 Cobra, this design featured twin vertical tail fins and was powered by two General Electric YF101 'leaky turbojet' engines.

tion of wing/fuselage blending, forebody strakes and canards, plus the number, planform and location of the tail surfaces.

Combat priorities laid down by the LWF requirements were turning performance at Mach 1·2 (demanding low wave drag), turning performance at Mach 0·9 (demanding optimum drag-at-lift), acceleration (requiring minimal wave drag) and maximum lift at Mach 0·8/40,000ft (12,000m) (again requiring optimum drag-at-lift). These conflicting

Below: In creating the production configuration (right), GD engineers slightly increased the dimensions of the original YF-16 (left), and reprofiled the nose section to accommodate the APG-66 radar. This photograph shows the second YF-16 and the first FSD aircraft.

demands made the selection of a wing planform difficult. In many ways, a straight wing fitted with leading edge flaps offered the best compromise, but wave drag was high. Wave drag of a swept wing would have been better, but penalties would have been paid in terms of handling qualities and drag-at-lift.

Previous fighters from the same design stable were the delta-winged F-102 Delta Dagger and F-106 Delta Dart, and the variable-geometry F-111, but neither of these proven technologies seemed right for the new fighter. Delta wings offer high volumetric efficiency, along with low structural weight and wave drag, but suffer penalties in trim drag and drag-at-lift. Variable geometry can give optimum aerodynamic performance in all flight conditions, but imposes problems at weight and balance.

The design finally adopted traded wing loading against aspect ratio to achieve the optimum balance between the conflicting demands imposed by the turn rate and acceleration requirements. Leading-edge sweep angles of 35deg, 40deg and 45deg were tested, along with six aerofoil sections. The

latter included constant thickness and camber, and designs in which these parameters were varied from root to tip. The selected design has a leading edge sweep of 40deg, an aspect ratio of 3·0 and a wing loading of 60lb/sq ft (2·53kg/sq m).

A wing of fixed camber could not have satisfied the conflicting demands of takeoff and landing, subsonic cruise, combat manoeuvring at high G levels and supersonic flight, but the use of variable camber played a major part in maintaining aircraft handling qualities and performance, particularly throughout the likely range of air combat speeds (Mach 0·8 to 1·6). It also allowed the use of a low aspect ratio and a thickness of only four per cent, factors which helped to optimize drag-at-lift and thus transonic manoeuvring.

To achieve this, the YF-16 wing was fitted with leading and trailing-edge flaps: if used throughout the flight envelope, these would help match the wing to changing Mach number and angle of attack. And instead of the slotted pattern of leading-edge flaps often used in other aircraft during takeoff and landing, the YF-16 wing incorporated a plain single-in-chord flap. Flap positions are automatically adjusted by the flight-control system.

Design similarities
At first sight, the competing GD and Northrop designs looked very different, but both made use of moderately swept wings and long root extensions. This was no coincidence, both teams having concluded that the vortexes cast by such extensions at high angles of attack would maintain a good airflow across the wing, even beyond stalling point, thus promising good handling at high angles of attack.

Another area of advanced technology in the YF-16 design was the adoption of wing-body blending. Near the root, the wing's depth is increased to the point where it blends smoothly into the fuselage. Company engineers had originally devised this technique in the late 1940s during studies of jet-powered seaplane fighters, though the definitive Convair YF2Y fighter which flew in 1953 did not in practice use wing-body blending.

Above: Formation take-off by the first and second full-scale development aircraft. The latter sports its third paint scheme – the all-grey finish which replaced the earlier blue-on-white and red/white/blue markings. Both aircraft are fitted with instrumented nose probes.

The technique was also used on the Douglas Skyray and Saab 35 Draken, in both cases providing sufficient internal volume for a substantial payload of fuel.

The YF-16 centre of gravity was located far enough aft to reduce longitudinal stability and increase manoeuvrability. Since lift acted ahead of the c.g., the tailplane was required to push the tail of the aircraft up rather than down in order to maintain level flight. It thus added to the lift rather than subtracting from it as on normal designs. At supersonic speeds, the centre of pressure moved aft, reducing the amount of downward force which the horizontal tail surfaces had to apply.

To 'tame' the resulting flying characteristics, the GD design team had to provide a full-time fly-by-wire stability augmentation and flight-control system to translate the pilot's control demands into movements of the aircraft control surfaces. Without the confidence gained with the YF-16, the Air Force probably would not have adopted a fly-by-wire control system in the production aircraft, a service project director stated in 1977.

In selecting an engine for the new fighter, the GD designers had to consider not only the virtues of single and twin-engined installations, but also the effects of different engine cycles (bypass ratio and pressure ratio). The most obvious candidates were a single Pratt & Whitney F100 or a pair of General Electric YF101s. The former was already under development for use in the F-15 Eagle, and its medium bypass-ratio turbofan design offered high thrust and good fuel economy.

The Fort Worth team did look into the possibility of creating a much lighter aircraft powered by a single YF101, but studies suggested that this would be unable to meet the performance requirements. This approach was in fact to

Right: Experimental 'lizard' camouflage scheme of dark grey, olive drab and dark green worn by two 388th TFW/16th TFTS F-16s, this one a two-seat F-16B, in 1979–80.

be adopted in the late 1970s by Northrop, when the latter company set out to create what eventually became the F-20 Tigershark, but this is a 'shorter-legged' design less able to carry out long-range bombing missions.

The safety factors involved in single and twin-engine designs are more difficult to quantify. Discussing this problem in a technical paper on YF-16 development, Deputy Program Director Harry Hillaker stated "Many evaluations of accumulated accident-rate data have been made with varying conclusions. The number of variables involved in these evaluations make it impossible to arrive at a specific conclusion. I will debate, however, the argument that safety is the primary consideration in determining the desired number of engines." The merits of single versus twin-engined designs are still a subject of debate, and one which was later to play a significant role in persuading some nations to adopt the twin-engined F-18 Hornet rather than the GD fighter.

First flights

The first YF-16 prototype was rolled out at Forth Worth on December 13, 1973, a mere 21 months after GD received the

$37·9 million contract. First flight of the YF-16 took place on January 20, 1974 at Edwards AFB – ahead of schedule and much to the surprise of GD pilot Phil Oestricher and all the technicians watching what should have been a high-speed taxi trial to check pitch and roll response.

As the aircraft gained speed and was rotated into a nose-up attitude, a diverging rolling oscillation built up. Distracted by this, and still relatively unfamiliar with the YF-16's high thrust-to-weight ratio, Oestricher allowed the speed to build up to around 150kt. Realizing that the horizontal tailplane had hit the runway, Oestricher decided that the best way of handling the problem was to get airborne. A brief six-minute circuit followed, and the YF-16 was successfully brought in to a smooth landing.

The subsequent investigation showed that the oscillation experienced during the roll down the runway had been pilot-induced, largely as a result of the gain of the flight-control system. The 'fix' was simple – the gain was reduced by 50 per cent while the aircraft was on the ground, then automatically raised to its full value once airborne.

Above: The moment of liftoff as the third FSD aircraft leaves the Forth Worth runway to begin an avionics test mission. The nose radome carries the normal pattern of probe, while the small black 'teardrop' fairing immediately behind the radome is for a radar-warning receiver.

The official first flight followed on February 2, with Oestricher once again at the controls. The prototype was taken up to 15,000ft (4,500m) with the undercarriage extended. The gear was then retracted, the speed increased to 300–350kt and 2–3g turns carried out. The sortie lasted for 90 minutes. Three days later, Oestricher took the aircraft supersonic for the first time, reaching a top speed of Mach 1·2 and remaining supersonic for five minutes. Manoeuvres at up to 5g were also carried out during this third flight of the YF-16.

By the time that the second prototype joined the programme in May of that year, temporary flying restrictions had been placed on the type following two incidents in which the F100 turbofan had lost power. Both were traced to contamination of the fuel-control valve which had caused this component to

Above: Near-plan view of the third FSD aircraft during a sortie from Edwards Air Force Base. The muzzle port for the 20mm M61 cannon is a prominent feature on the port-side strake. The black-and-white film used has increased the contrast of non-standard markings.

jam at the idle position, but until the problem was cleared up the YF-16 had to remain within 'dead-stick' landing distance of the runway.

To allow spinning and spin-recovery characteristics to be safely explored, along with handling at high angles of attack, a 0·3-scale flying model was flown at Edwards AFB in 1975. Built from glass fibre with an aluminium sub-structure, this was 14ft (4·27m) long, had an 8ft 9in (2·67m) wingspan and was stressed to handle loads of up to 5·5g.

Below: Delivered in November 1977, FSD aircraft No 5 was initially used to explore aircraft handling qualities. It was later assigned to Eglin Air Force Base in Florida to take part in Seek Eagle – a USAF programme to determine the limits of the F-16's weapons carrying capability.

An operational fighter

Even before the second prototype had flown, the LWF programme was no longer just a technology demonstration. In April 1974 US Defense Secretary James R. Schlesinger decided that the successful LWF contender was to be developed into an operational type designated ACF (Air Combat Fighter). As flight testing of the YF-16 and the rival YF-17 continued throughout 1974, pilots from the USAF, US Navy and US government were able to evaluate both types. Trials included air-to-air combat against the A-37B Dragonfly, F-106 Delta Dart, F-4 Phantom and MiG-21. These tests were completed by the end of 1974.

Selection of the YF-16 was announced on January 13, 1975. Secretary of the Air Force John McLucas stated that performance of the GD aircraft had been 'significantly better' during the fly-off, particularly at supersonic and near-supersonic speeds. The YF-16 had also exhibited better acceleration, endurance and turning capability.

An initial development contract awarded by the USAF covered 15 development aircraft – 11 single-seat fighters and four two-seat trainers – and was worth $417.9 million. A separate $55.5 million contract to Pratt & Whitney covered engine development.

The production aircraft was effectively a slightly scaled-up version of the prototype design. The latter had not been fitted with nose radars, and original USAF planning had assumed that the ACF design would carry a small search radar similar in peformance to the Emerson APQ-159 fitted to the Northrop F-5E. The subsequent decision to adopt a more powerful multi-mode set required an increase in nose volume, nose length being extended by 7in (17·8cm), while nose diameter was increased by 4in (10·2cm). The number of access doors on the airframe was increased in the revised design, while the number of weapon stations was increased from seven to nine.

Selection of the YF-16 ended any chance that four NATO countries – Belgium, Denmark, the Netherlands and Norway, all of which were looking to replace their F-104 Starfighters – might adopt the YF-17, although Northrop pointed out that their design had been flown with prototype engines which had clocked up less than 1,000 hours of test running. Production engines would have provided eight per cent more

thrust, raising aircraft performance.

The USAF concluded that the GD aircraft outperformed the Northrop design in several areas, although the latter was superior in some respects. Around Mach 0·7, the YF-17 could outturn the YF-16, but from Mach 0·8 upwards the YF-16 was better. The GD aircraft had greater range, and was considered to be closer in standard to a production design in terms of weight, fuel capacity, and thrust-to-weight ratio.

USAF studies suggested that flyaway costs of the F-16 would be some six to seven per cent lower than those of the F-17, and that savings could also be anticipated in development and operation. Engine choice was not a factor in the selection, but the twin-engined design would have consumed 20 per cent more fuel, an important factor as the price of oil continued to rise following the 1973 Middle East War.

US Navy interest

In the meantime, the GD aircraft remained a contender for the US Navy's contemporary NACF (Navy Air Combat Fighter) programme to replace the F-4 Phantom and A-7 Corsair. One configuration proposed by the Fort Worth team was a single-seat design using the fuselage of the two-seat trainer in order to obtain more internal volume for avionics or fuel. The YF-16 had 18cu ft (0·51cu m) of volume for internal avionics, a figure which was reduced in practice to 12·8cu ft (0·36cu m) by the installation of flight test avionics. The new proposal

Above: An international quartet poses on a snow-cleared taxiway – production F-16s in the markings of Norway (bottom left), Netherlands (upper left), Belgium (upper right) and Denmark (bottom right). All are two-seat F-16B versions.

would have provided up to 25cu ft (0·71cu m) of space.

The four NATO nations sent a delegation to the US in May 1974 to discuss possible LWF procurement. At that time the USAF were thinking of ordering 650 fighters, with the US Navy taking a further 800 examples. Selection of the USAF's new fighter was not scheduled until May 1975, but the European air arms wanted a decision by the end of September 1974.

This date was impossible to attain, but the deadline for USAF source selection was brought forward to January 1975 by speeding up the flight test programme. Flight refuelling was used to extend the duration of individual flight-test sorties, while the programme was revamped to avoid unnecessary duplication of flight test conditions. Instead of the two and half years normally required to complete Category 3 flight testing on a new aircraft, the YF-16 and -17 tests were completed in sufficient detail to allow source selection in January 1975, barely a year after first flight. At this point the US Navy, considering that it did not have sufficient data to make a choice, quit the LWF programme to continue its own studies of both aircraft.

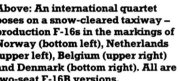

Meanwhile the deadline for submission of proposals to the NATO Governments had been extended to January 1975 at the request of the US. The formal F-16 proposal was submitted on January 14, a day after the Swedish proposal (for the SAAB-Scania 37E Viggen) and a day ahead of the French (for the M53 turbofan-powered Dassault-Breguet Mirage F.1E).

The formal decision to adopt the F-16 came as no surprise when announced on June 7, 1975, although many observers noted that Belgium planned to deploy 102 aircraft rather than the anticipated 116. The resulting cost savings were intended to be invested in research and development work directed towards a new West European combat aircraft.

F-16 production

In developing the F-16 from the YF-16, changes were kept to a minimum. Fuselage length was extended by 10in (25·4cm), while the wing area was increased by 20sq ft (1·85sq m), and fitted with two additional hard points. The horizontal tailplane was increased in size, and a jet starter was added to the F100 turbofan.

Assembly of the first full-scale production F-16 began in December 1975, and involved GD in a major modernization of its Fort Worth plant. Since the F-111 programme, the latter (officially USAF Plant 4) had been under-utilized, and had seen no major investment or updating since the 1960s. GD initially hoped to get Department of Defense funding for the modernization needed for the F-16 programme, but the US Government had already decided that it was no longer prepared to finance capital facilities needed for military projects. The Pentagon agreed that the plant would require updating, but expected GD to finance this themselves. By the summer of 1982 the company had invested $70 million, and was planning to spend $25 million more.

In laying out the production line, GD allowed for production of up to 45 aircraft per month. By the end of 1980, production was running at 16 per month and the manufacturer estimated that the current tooling could be used to build another 23–25 per month if required.

Under the 1975 agreement, a total of 348 F-16s for the European partners were to be assembled in Europe, 184 at the Fokker plant at Schiphol in the Netherlands, and 164 by SABCA at Gosselies in Belgium. The four nations are also entitled to offsets of 10 per cent of the dollar value of each aircraft sold to the USAF, and 15 per cent on aircraft sold to other export customers.

The Memorandum of Understanding covering European purchase and co-production of the F-16 ensured that the European companies involved in the project would receive work not only on USAF aircraft but also on Fighting Falcons built for Third World operators. It also stipulated the payment to the US government of a $471,000 research and development levy on the price of each aircraft delivered to the four air arms. The latter figure includes a recoupment charge for F100 R & D.

Preliminary contracts for the F-16 were placed in 1975 with European industry. It is impractical to detail all the suppliers in a programme of this mag-

Left: Demonstration flight by two brand new F-16As of the USAF. In the clean configuration shown here the aircraft could easily outfly the MiG-21 and could probably cope with the new MiG-29 Fulcrum. These particular Fighting Falcons were delivered in April 1980.

Above: F-16s on the final assembly line at Fokker's Schipol plant in the Netherlands. Co-ordination and control of the multi-national assembly programme was a formidable management task comparable to that of the Apollo space programme.

nitude, but the main contracts were awarded as follows.

Two aircraft assembly lines were set up, one at the SABCA plant at Gosselies in Belgium, where Belgian and Danish airframes are assembled, the other at the Fokker plant at Schiphol-Oost in the Netherlands. At the same time, the Belgian company SONACA – formerly Fairey SA – was reconstituted with new management and was contracted to build the aft fuselage.

Assembly of aircraft for the Netherlands and Norway is handled by Fokker, who also build the centre fuselage, the leading edge flaps, the trailing edge panel and flaperon. SABCA facilities at Gosselies and Haren in Belgium tackle the wing structure box and assembly of the complete wing. Other components such as the vertical fin box and the wing and centreline pylons are built in Denmark by Per Udsen, while the undercarriage is tackled by DAF in the Netherlands, and the wheels by Raufoss in Norway.

European assembly of the F100 engine is handled by the Belgian company Fabrique Nationale, which invested around $35 million in new test cells, machine tools and other equipment. Kongsberg builds the engine fan-drive turbine module in Norway, while Phillips in Holland is responsible for the augmentor nozzle module.

Contracts for avionics are widely scattered throughout the four nations. MBLE (Belgium) has overall responsibility for the APG-66 radar, while Signaal and Oldelft (Netherlands) are responsible for the radar antennae and HUDs respectively. Also involved in HUD work are Marconi Avionics in Britain (the original designer of the unit) and Kongsberg. Danish Industrial Group One (Neselco and LK-NES) supply the fire-control computer, the radar displays are built by Danish company Nea Linberg, and Kongsberg handles the inertial navigation system as well as its other contributions.

The creation of European F-16 production facilities was not an easy task. European industry had earlier built the Lockheed F-104G Starfighter, but the latter aircraft was not in USAF service. Since the F-16 is a front-line US warplane, and would be assembled on both sides of the Atlantic, many procedures had to be agreed, standardized and in some cases made the subject of compromise. In the early days of the YF-16 project, paperwork had been kept to a minimum in order to maintain the pace of the programme, but with the adoption of the F-16 by four NATO nations, Fighting Falcon became what is probably the most complex management task that the US Department of Defense has ever undertaken. In 1977 programme director Brigadier General James Abrahamson described the task he faced as "a management nightmare". More than 3,000 suppliers and sub-contractors were involved in the international programme, and even under the 998-aircraft production run originally planned some 20,000,000lb

(9,000,000kg) of raw material and three million individual manufactured items were due to cross the Atlantic.

In an ideal world, the F-16 would not have been committed to large-scale overseas production until the design had been frozen and proven, and until the Fort Worth line had ironed out the inevitable production 'bugs'. In practice, however, the aircraft entered production on a similar timescale in both the US and Western Europe, with production facilities being planned before the design was fully refined or production techniques checked out. Not since the days of the original US ICBM programmes had such pressures been placed on project management.

Project management

Since the programme involved contractors in five nations, it was essential to set up procedures under which proposed changes to the design could be jointly discussed and agreed, so that a common standard of hardware would be produced by all of the nations involved. Before components and aircraft could be built, technical standards, acceptance procedures, working practices and even accounting methods had to be jointly agreed. In some cases fundamental differences in procedure and outlook were uncovered.

The US aerospace worker is mobile in outlook, and will tend to 'follow the contracts', working for whatever company needs his services. Two-shift production working is common on large programmes, maintaining production speed and helping to amortize the cost of expensive tooling. In Western Europe, staff are less mobile, with companies placing greater emphasis on long-term workload, and providing greater job security for their employees. Single-shift working is normal, and expensive overtime often frowned upon. It is not uncommon for aerospace plants to shut down completely for anything up to a month during the holiday period.

Such practices may be thought desirable in Europe, but they penalized the performance of the many non-US F-16 contractors. In 1977 it was estimated that European co-production would add over a million dollars to the cost of each F-16 purchased by the NATO air arms. A penalty was also paid in terms of time. As production began, GD estimated the lead time on its Fort Worth line as 24 months, while in the case of the European assembly lines, this rose to 36 months.

In both cases, the end result was increased cost. Unit flyaway price of a USAF F-16 was originally set at $4·55 million in 1975 dollars. The price tag agreed for the NATO aircraft was $6·09 million. Part of this increase was due to R&D levy of $470,000 per aircraft, but the remainder was a reflection of the increased tooling costs and longer lead times.

Methods by which US aerospace suppliers added fixed charges to production costs in order to recover administration and other overhead costs had all been devised to cope with production carried out mostly in the US by US companies. In instances where raw parts might be fabricated in the US, shipped to Europe for finishing, then returned to the US for incorporation within USAF aircraft, normal procedures became distinctly cumbersome.

Above: F-16 centre-fuselage sections on the production line at Fokker's Ypenburg plant in the Netherlands. These sections show how wing/body blending was used by GD engineers in creating the F-16. The central tunnel houses the F100 turbofan.

European co-production

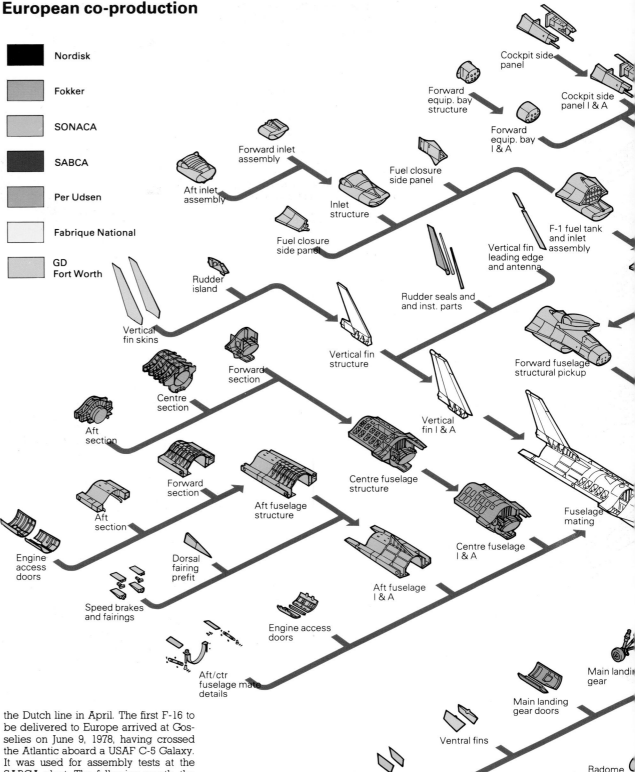

- Nordisk
- Fokker
- SONACA
- SABCA
- Per Udsen
- Fabrique National
- GD Fort Worth

Bookkeeping was further complicated by the fact that US procurement procedures dictate that the financial records of companies supplying defence hardware be officially audited, but the European companies involved in F-16 assembly were, not unnaturally, reluctant to allow the US government access to detailed financial data. A compromise was devised under which the individual companies were checked by auditors from their own national governments.

Late in 1976, the smooth running of the programme was disrupted when the USAF decided to standardize on the McDonnell Douglas ACES 11 ejection seat without fully consulting the West Europeans.

The NATO air arms requested a total of 18 changes to the F-16. Seven were subsequently cancelled, six were adopted by all five operators and decisions on five more were deferred. These NATO requests added useful facilities to the aircraft, including:
* improvements to the radar to suppress the effects of sea clutter, and to allow a radar image to be 'frozen' on the display
* navigation update capability
* an altitude-hold facility in the aircraft autopilot
* installation of a radar electro-optical video recorder
* improved anti-corrosion treatment

Despite such problems, and the inevitable political haggling over the distribution of offset work, the programme flowed smoothly during the second half of the 1970s. First European co-production contracts were formally signed in July 1976, and the following October saw the first full-scale development aircraft rolled out at Forth Worth, with the first flight following in December.

Full-scale production

The third full-scale development aircraft was used for avionics testing. The radar was delivered two months later, but came with an unexpected bonus - it incorporated a more advanced standard of hardware and software than had been planned - and did not affect the timescale of avionics flight testing.

At the start of 1977 the USAF announced plans to purchase an additional 738 aircraft. Formal authority for full-scale production was given the following October, two months after the first two-seat F-16B flew.

By February 1978 the Belgian production line had opened, followed by

the Dutch line in April. The first F-16 to be delivered to Europe arrived at Gosselies on June 9, 1978, having crossed the Atlantic aboard a USAF C-5 Galaxy. It was used for assembly tests at the SABCA plant. The following month, the first European-built F-16 components - a set of wings - were fitted to a USAF aircraft on the Fort Worth line. The two-way flow of components across the Atlantic had become a reality.

Meanwhile, in the spring of 1978, the US General Accounting Office published a report on the F-16 which drew attention to a number of development problems, including engine malfunctions, structural cracks, minor problems with the radar, and instability at high angles of attack. The report called for the review of the programme and the likely threats which the aircraft would face in service, but pointed out that the problems met to date '... do not seem to be any more severe than those previously experienced in other major systems. And experience with the systems shows that these problems are resolved over time'.

This report attracted some unfavourable publicity for the type, with several knocking reports appearing in print and on TV, but these overlooked the fact that the GAO was to some degree reporting past history. Fixes to many

problems were already at hand.

First flight of a production aircraft from the Fort Worth line took place in August 1978, with the maiden flight of a European F-16 following on December 11, 1978, from Gosselies. This was a two-seat F-16B, and was flown by Neil Anderson and Serge Martin, the latter having spent two weeks on familiarization training at Forth Worth prior to the historic sortie.

Deliveries to the user air arms started in January 1979 when aircraft were delivered from US and European production lines to the 388th TFW at Hill AFB, Utah, and to the FAéB (Force Aérienne Belge, or Belgian Air Force) respectively. In May the first Fokker-built aircraft flew, and four US aircraft completed a four-month series of tests in Europe. A month later the KLu (Koninklijke Luchtmacht, or Royal

Netherlands Air Force) accepted its first F-16s, and in January 1980 deliveries began to the air arms of Denmark, Norway and Israel.

By the end of 1979, the unit flyaway cost of the F-16A was $10.2 million. In numerical terms this may have been far above the $3.0 million originally envisaged back in 1972, but in 1975 dollars was around $4.7 million - well below the USAF 1975 target price of $5.0 million. Until 1980, the F-16 lacked a name. The unofficial use of 'Falcon' resulted in objections by Dassault-Breguet who already used the name for their range of business jets. At a time when the USAF was re-using Second World War nomenclature, the F-16's high performance, long range, bubble canopy and ventral air inlet suggested 'Mustang II' to may observers, but this had been pre-empted by an automobile manufac-

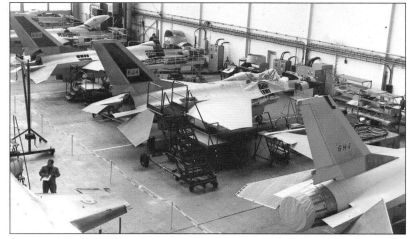

Right: The second European F-16 assembly line is at the SABCA plant at Gosselies, Belgium. Deliveries to the air arms of Belgium and Denmark started in January 1979.

Below: This flow chart shows the principal structural assemblies of European-built F-16s and identifies the major suppliers. The use of European and American components in aircraft built on both sides of the Atlantic involved an immense administrative effort, and European industrial practices were largely responsible for each locally-built NATO aircraft costing a million dollars more than the USAF equivalent. I & A indicates Integration and Assembly.

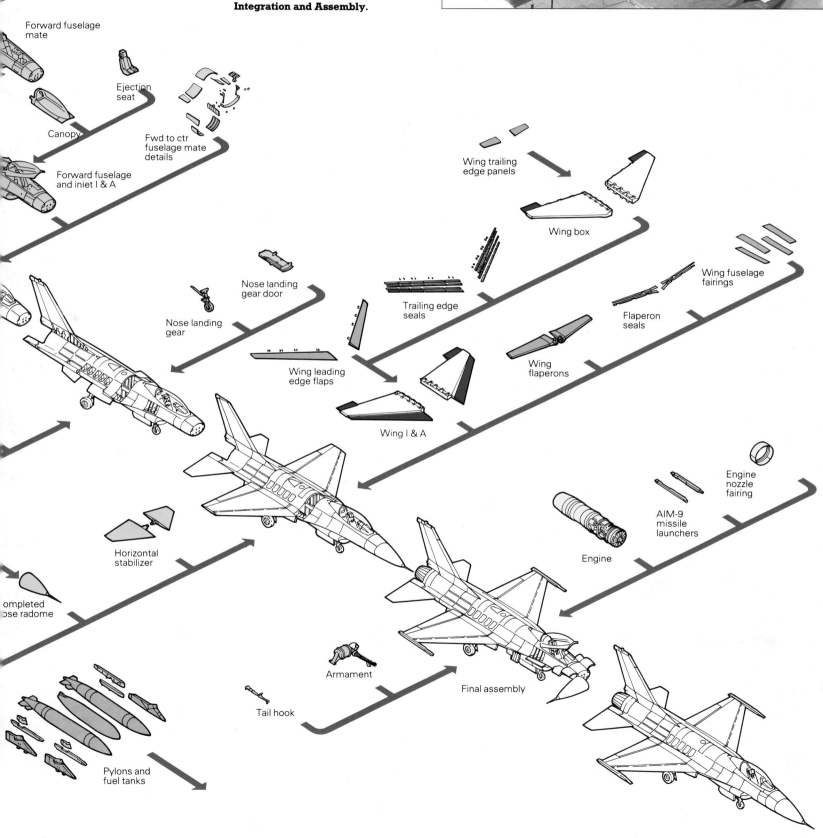

Cockpit structure

Forward fuselage mate

Ejection seat

Canopy

Fwd to ctr fuselage mate details

Forward fuselage and inlet I & A

Wing trailing edge panels

Wing box

Nose landing gear door

Nose landing gear

Trailing edge seals

Wing fuselage fairings

Flaperon seals

Wing leading edge flaps

Wing flaperons

Wing I & A

Engine nozzle fairing

AIM-9 missile launchers

Horizontal stabilizer

Engine

Completed nose radome

Armament

Tail hook

Final assembly

Pylons and fuel tanks

turer. Final choice, made in 1980, was the unimaginative 'Fighting Falcon'.

First phase of the F-16 Operational Test and Evaluation programme was carried out at Hill AFB, Utah, but this was followed by international trials. Nine aircraft took part in the MOTE (Multinational Operational Test & Evaluation) programme, including two from the Belgian and Netherland Air Forces. Six aircraft, plus one of the two reserves and more than 120 personnel, spent six weeks in each of the participating nations during the second half of 1980, so that operating experience could be built up.

The F-16/79 export fighter

In the first weeks of 1980 a new shape was given to future US fighter exports when President Carter reversed his 1977 decision that the development of military aircraft specifically for the export market would not be allowed. The guidelines laid down for the proposed FX export fighter called for performance and cost to be between those of the F-5E and the F-16A.

Designs were to be multirole, but optimized for air-to-air combat and with deliberately restricted strike capability. Payload/range performance had to be clearly inferior to that of current front-line types, but deployment and maintenance had to be easier, and the new fighters must not be easily upgradable without US permission. Finally, development of FX fighters was to be a commercial undertaking by the companies concerned, who had to accept all marketing and financial risks. The two obvious candidates were GD with a down-rated derivative of the F-16, and Northrop with its new F-5G single-engined member of the Freedom Fighter/Tiger II family.

In order to create the resulting F-16/79 prototype, GD acquired a two-seat F-16B from the USAF in June 1980. The aircraft supplied was 75-0752, one of the original pair of full-scale development F-16Bs. General Electric created a new J79-GE-17X version of this, well-proven single-shaft engine specifically for the project, modifying it to match the F-16 airframe and to give a useful amount of extra thrust.

To keep airframe modifications to a minimum, the J79 installation locates the front face of the engine compressor in a similar location to that of the compressor face in the F100-powered aircraft. Since the GE engine is 18in (46cm) longer than the F100, the rear fuselage has had to be extended aft of the taileron pivot point by an equivalent amount.

The GE turbojet requires a lower airflow than the F100, so GD devised a new pattern of intake. The standard intake had been designed as a single removable component, which made substitution of the new version an easy job. The new unit looks externally similar to the original, but the upper surface extends much further forward, making an easy recognition feature. This new intake incorporates a fixed compression ramp in its roof, and a bypass valve designed to supply a flow of cooling air to the engine bay.

A steel heat shield weighing almost 2,000lb (900kg) surrounds most of the length of the new engine, and accounts for most of the increased structural weight of the new version. This protects the structure of the aft fuselage from the high level of heat generated by the turbojet. Being a turbofan, the F100 passes relatively cool air from the fan along a duct just below the outer casing, consequently radiating less heat.

Private venture

Like the rival Northrop F-20, the F-16/79 was developed as a private venture. Total cost of construction and flight test – some $18 million according to a GD estimate – was shared by the airframe and engine manufacturers. Unit flyaway cost was $8·0 million in 1980 prices.

Being only a minimal change from the standard aircraft, the F-16/79 required no new fatigue or other structural testing, and its assembly could be fitted easily into the normal Fort Worth line. Single and two-seat F-16/79 models were planned, and GD intended to begin deliveries to a customer two years after signing the letter of authorization.

The conversion task was quickly accomplished, and the single F-16/79 prototype flew for the first time on October 29, 1980. By early June of the following year it had clocked up a total of 122 flying hours in 131 sorties, demonstrating a top speed of Mach 2·0 and and altitude of 50,000ft (15,000m) along with 9g manoeuvres. The first flights were naturally for trials purposes, but evaluation flights followed, and by July 1981 28 pilots had flown the aircraft. These included GD personnel and pilots from the USAF, USN and three foreign air forces.

The formal US Department of Defense policy on FX was spelled out in the autumn of 1982, days before Northrop rolled out the F-20 prototype, in a letter from Deputy Defense Secretary Frank Carlucci to Air Force Secretary Verne Orr and Navy Secretary John Lehman. "There are several friends and

allies that are now, or soon will be, engaged in the process of modernizing their respective tactical air forces. Only a few can afford first-line fighters, and because of fiscal and other restraints it is important that the United States has alternatives to front-line aircraft available for export.

"The alternative is the FX either as a stand-alone capability or as an element of lo/hi mix. It is clearly in the US national security interest to have our friends and allies equipped with systems that will still be militarily capable in the late 1980s and into the 1990s.

"For this reason, we must selectively but actively encourage the foreign procurement of the FX, not leave this marketing effort just to the manufacturers. Wherever possible and appropriate, your departments will encourage representatives of foreign governments and defence establishments to include the FX in their aircraft modernization plans."

Countries identified as potential FX customers are Bahrain, Egypt, Indonesia, Jordan, Malaysia, Oman, Philippines, Saudi Arabia, Thailand, Turkey and United Arab Emirates. Sales

Above: Even if the tail markings had been omitted, the extended jet pipe and modified inlets on this two-seater would identify it as an F-16/79.

Right: The F-16/79 was developed as an FX-class export fighter, but the concept was never really viable once the standard F100-powered aircraft was cleared for general export. No-one was prepared to pay large sums of money for a downgraded plane.

of FX will also be promoted in South America. GD salesmen predicted that up to 20 air arms were potential customers for the F-16/79 and that as many as 1,000 aircraft might be built. Nations briefed on the F-16/79 included Austria, Jordan, Malaysia, Nigeria, Singapore, Taiwan and Thailand.

The idea of marketing a downgraded warplane may have made sense to the Carter administration, but potential customers were unimpressed. In 1984 Singapore became the first and only customer for the F-16/79, but a year later was allowed to buy the standard F-16 instead.

The F-16/101

While the F-16/79 was taking part in a highly-publicized test programme, GD was also testing a second re-engined version of the Fighting Falcon. On December 19, 1980, GD flew the first F-16 to be powered by the General Electric F110 turbofan. Originally known as the F101 DFE (Derivative Fighter Engine), this was an experimental engine intended to maintain GE design expertise in the field of high-thrust afterburning turbofans and to be a possible new engine for the F-14 Tomcat and F-16.

F-16/101 flight testing went smoothly, all trials objectives being accomplished by May 29 of the following year in 58 sorties and 75 flying hours – 25 hours less than planned. Twelve pilots flew the aircraft during a programme of development trials which included close-support, strike and air-to-air missions. The only major incident which marred this fast-moving and successful test programme was a single dead-stick landing in January 1981 due to a fuel leak.

Staged improvements

While development of the F-16/79 was being carried out, work on other versions continued. The Fighting Falcon finally achieved Initial Operating Capability (IOC) with the USAF in November 1980, while in January 1981 349 squadron of the Belgian air force became the first F-16 unit to qualify for NATO service in Europe.

A project as large as the F-16 is certain to attract critics. The most common complaint levelled by its detractors, particularly in the earliest stages of the full-scale development programme, was that what started out as a cheap and simple lightweight fighter had grown into a complex and considerably heavier multirole design. To confuse the issue further, a second school of thought claimed that the aircraft and its systems were too simple, and that the Fighting Falcon would have difficulty in operating effectively in Western Europe's often-foul weather.

Simple day fighters of the type originally conceived by the 1972 Lightweight Fighter programme do have a useful operational role, but almost certainly not on NATO's Central Front. The general trend of USAF thinking has been that future version of the F-16 would need more sophisticated systems in order to fight and survive in any 1980s conflict. To create and phase in such new equipment with a minimum of disruption to the Fighting Falcon production programme, the USAF and its NATO allies have devised the Multinational Staged Improvement Programme (MSIP). This will add improvements in a gradual manner.

The first MSIP Phase 1 aircraft was USAF aircraft no 330, which entered final assembly in the summer of 1981. The NATO consortium introduced the same build standard early in 1982.

Also known as F-16+, the MSIP Phase 1 standard incorporates Engineering Change Proposal 0350, which adds the structural changes and new wiring required by beyond-visual range (BVR) AMRAAM missiles, electro-optical nav/attack systems, internal ECM and other new avionics. A further modification, ECP 0425, involves increasing the size of the horizontal tail, in order to increase the surface's ability to cope with changes of c.g caused by heavy weapon loads. Tail surface area is increased by 30 per cent over the 49sq ft (4·55sq m) of earlier aircraft, empty weight being increased by around 200lb (90kg) as a result. The original component used a titanium pivot shaft and sub-spar, but the opportunity was

Above: First Fighting Falcon to use the General Electric F110 turbofan (formerly the F101 Derivative Fighter Engine) was the F-16/101. The F110 was developed from the F101 powerplant of the B-1 bomber.

Below: Seen parked on the ramp at its home base of NAS Jacksonville, Florida, this F-16B two-seater trainer displays the distinctive lightning bolt unit marking of the 159th FIS, Florida ANG.

taken to eliminate this expensive material for the stabilizer. This decision reflected a dramatic increase in the cost of titanium in the late 1970s following the Soviet cutback in exports of the metal.

Under the Pacer Loft programme the European F-16 fleet is being modified to match the USAF standard.

External differences

The most obvious external sign of Pacer Loft is a grey camouflage finish on the nose radome in place of the earlier black. A new pattern of canopy is physically interchangeable with those on other F-16s, but the remaining improvements are all internal. These include changes intended to cure potential minor problems detected during early service experience. Rain water had been observed accumulating at some locations within the structure, so drainage holes have been drilled in the forward fuselage area and vertical fin. Maximum takeoff weight is increased

FLORIDA AIR NATIONAL GUARD

from 35,500lb (16,103kg) to 37,000lb (16,783kg), while the all-up weight for 9g manoeuvres has risen from 22,500lb (10,206kg) to 25,300lb (11.476kg).

Production of MSIP I aircraft (known as Block 15) started in late 1981. These MSIP I changes added approximately 200lb (90kg) to aircraft weight.

MSIP II took the development process a stage further. The Block 25 aircraft introduced in the second half of 1984 had a new APG-68 radar, a wide-angle HUD, two new multimode CRT cockpit displays, facilities for the AGM-65D Imaging Infra-Red (IIR) version of the Maverick air-to-surface missile, plus a new digital fly-by-wire system which replaced the earlier analogue model.

These extensive changes warranted a new designation – F-16C (single-seat) and -16D (two-seat). Although the aircraft has since seen other changes, these did not rival the complexity of MSIP II, so the C and D designations remain in use.

The next change was a revised engine bay able to accept two patterns of

engine – the latest 23,770lb (10,780kg) thrust F100-PW-220 or the new General Electric F110-GE-100. Rated at 28,982lb (13,146kg) thrust, the GE engine was based on the F101/DFE tested in 1980/81.

Production deliveries of this new version started in mid-1986. Aircraft fitted with the P&W engine were designated Block 30, while those with the more powerful GE engine became Block 32.

To provide the increased airflow demanded by the new engine, the GE-powered aircraft have a larger intake. This apparently simple modification created stability problems when the aircraft was flown at high angles of attack with a 300-gallon (1,135-litre) centreline tank in place. Changes to the aircraft's yaw limiter finally cleared the problem, and a retrofit scheme was applied to the F-16C/D fleet.

Other Block 30/32 changes included seal-bond tanks, computer memory expansion, plus provision for two new missiles – the Texas Instruments AGM-45 Shrike anti-radiation missile (ARM) and the new Hughes AIM-120A AMRAAM.

The older F-16A and B were still being built for export, and in 1987 the Block 15 OCU (Operational Capability Upgrade) model added the F100-PW-220 engine, a radar altimeter, expanded computer, wide-angle HUD – as used in F-15C/D – provision for the Atlis II electro-optical pod, plus provision for the Kongsberg Penguin anti-ship missile and beyond-visual range missiles such as the AIM-7 Sparrow or AIM-120A AMRAAM.

Production of this version is expected to run until 1996. Under a modification programme begun in 1987, some USAF and export Block 10 and Block 15 are being upgraded to Block 15 OCU standard.

Another late-1980s F-16A/B variant was built not by GD but at the Ogden Air Logistic Center, at Hill AFB, Utah. To provide the US Air National Guard with new interceptors, a batch of 279 existing F-16A was rebuilt to the Block 15 ADF standard. This $279 million programme added new Sparrow/AMRAAM compatible launch rail on underwing hardpoints 3 and 7, a night-identification searchlight mounted in the left forward nose area, Have Quick II secure radio, a GPS satnav receiver, and a survivable flight-data recorder. Additional electrical wiring has been added for this new hardware, also increased avionics cooling.

The radar was also modified for use with these radar-guided medium-range missiles, receiving a CW illuminator, null filler and tuning antennae which work with the Sparrow guidance system, updated software, and more computer memory. The stores-management computer was also given new software.

Conversion started in 1989 and was expected to run until 1992. A follow-on programme known as Falcon Sweep added the new Teledyne Advanced IFF (AIFF) interrogator, HF radio, and the USAF's new Combined Altitude Radar Altimeter (CARA).

By the time that the ANG was receiving its first Block 15 ADF aircraft, another new model was leaving the Fort Worth production line. Introduced in late 1988, this was designated Block 40/42, again depending on whether the GE or P&W engine was fitted. This version is equipped with the improved APG-68V radar. It also has interfaces for the LANTIRN electro-optical nav-attack pods, a LANTIRN-compatible wide-angle HUD based on diffractive optics and incorporating an enhanced envelope gunsight designed to improve kill capability during high-aspect engagements.

Other changes include an expanded

Right: Jet pipes of the F110-powered (left) and standard F100-powered (right) versions of the F-16.

Below: Fighting Falcon has now flown with the GE J79 turbojet, GE F110 (formerly F101 DFE) turbofan and the standard P&W F100 turbofan.

(256K) fire-control computer, a GPS satnav system, a four-channel digital fly-by-wire flight control system, plus the ability to carry AGM-88A HARM anti-radiation missiles. A total of 450 will be built. Block 40/42 aircraft have a strengthened wing and landing gear, are also able to operate at higher take-off weights.

The USAF urgently wanted these new features, so decided to accept the Block 40 aircraft into service long before testing and evaluation at Edwards AFB had been completed. Transition to the new model at the Fort Worth production line in 1988/89 took around six months, and did not go smoothly. By mid-1989, the company was almost 20 aircraft behind schedule. For the next two years, delays and quality-control problems were to plague the programme. These may have been due in part to skilled personnel being switched from the F-16 project to the US Navy's ill-fated A-12 Avenger II Advanced Tactical Aircraft. The latter was finally cancelled late in 1990.

In 1992 the delivery of the first Block 50/52 aircraft will take place. These will be fitted with uprated versions of the rival GE and P&W engines. Maximum thrust of the F100-PW-229 and F110-GE-129 will be around 29,000lb (13,150kg).

Avionics changes will include the improved APG-68(V5) radar, a 256K General Avionics Computer, a wide-angle HUD, a GPS satellite-navigation receiver, a ring-laser gyro INS, and an advanced RWR. These aircraft will be able to carry the new HARM III missile. In 1993 they will receive the new ALE-47 chaff/flare dispenser and the ASPJ EW system, also an Improved Data Modem data link for Harm/Shrike launch co-ordination, plus an On-Board Oxygen Generation System (OBOGS) able to process engine bleed air to enrich its oxygen concentration.

Plans for a proposed Block 60 version of the aircraft are not yet finalised. Features might include a head-steered FLIR, helmet-mounted displays and new digital avionics.

In the 1990s, the USAF hopes to field a replacement for the Fairchild A-10. Several designs were considered – including the F100-powered LTV YF-7F – but in late 1990 the USAF selected the A-16, a version of the F-16 fitted with new attack avionics. The build standard of the A-16 had not been defined, but GD suggested a head-steered FLIR system, the GPU-5/A Pave Penny EO pod, digital terrain-reference navigation for terrain avoidance, a GPS satnav receiver, plus a datalink to allow forward air controllers to input target co-ordinated information directly into the aircraft navigation system. Some ballistic hardening of the aircraft is also anticipated.

Plans to build the A-16 proved short-lived. Instead, the USAF intends to modify most of the Block 30 F-16C and D aircraft for the close support role, adding the planned A-16 avionics, plus a GAU-5 30mm gun pod. Modification kits are due to become available by the mid-1990s, the rebuild of 300 or more aircraft taking until around the end of the decade.

Initial rebuilds may not include the proposed FLIR, since development work on this had yet to start, and the USAF had not decided whether the system could be internally mounted or carried in a pod. Competitive evaluation of rival systems was planned, with selection of the winning design in late 1991 or early 1992. In practice, potential sensors had already been tested by the Service and by industry.

GD has carried out its own studies into possible EO sensors such as night-vision goggles, and navigation/attack FLIR systems such as the Hughes TINS used on night-attack F-18s, the Martin-Marietta Pathfinder system used on some Egyptian F-16s, GEC Avionics' Atlantic nav/attack FLIR pod, and the Flacon Eye second-generation FLIR.

Falcon Eye uses optics mounted in a MiG-29-style spherical housing located just ahead of the canopy to feed information to a helmet mounted display. Two magnifications are available; X1 for normal use and an X5.6 zoom.

Structure

In designing the structure of the F-16, General Dynamics engineers never lost sight of the fact that the end product must be easy to produce. Wherever possible, the attractions of advanced constructional methods such as chemical milling and exotic materials such as titanium and carbon-fibre composites were rejected. Without compromising the performance of the aircraft, the GD team created hardware which would eventually be assembled on three production lines by Belgian, Dutch and US workers, using components built to a common standard by sub-contractors on both sides of the Atlantic.

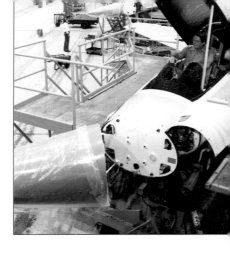

Fighting Falcon may be a high-performance aircraft of advanced aerodynamic form, but in designing its structure the GD engineers eschewed wherever possible sophisticated constructional techniques and materials. The USAF wanted an inexpensive fighter, so a modularized and simplified structural design was adopted.

Despite the aircraft's high performance, some 80 per cent of the structure is manufactured from aluminium alloy. A little less than 8 per cent is made from steel, composites account for less than 3 per cent, and titanium for a mere 1.5 per cent. Around 60 per cent of the structural parts are made from sheet metal, while less than 2 per cent require chemical milling.

The weight savings resulting from the use of advanced technology such as relaxed stability and wing/body blending are very significant, resulting in an empty weight some 1,300lb (590kg) less than would have been the case with a more conventional design. During full-scale development, GD estimated the cost of the F-16 airframe structure as $60 per lb, so this reduction in theory reduced airframe costs by around $80,000.

The development of a military aircraft is often a long saga of ever-increasing takeoff weight. This problem had dogged the F-111, the previous Fort Worth design, but in engineering the production F-16 the GD team maintained rigorous control over weight growth. Between April 1975 and January 1978 the takeoff weight increased by just over 5 per cent from 22,171lb (10,068kg) to 23,357lb (10,595kg), but more than half of this 'fat' reflected increased operational capability, producibility or maintainability.

Fatigue tests

In parallel with the flight-test programme a series of ground fatigue trials were carried out on the fifth development airframe. A test rig set up in a hangar at Fort Worth used more than 100 hydraulic rams to apply stress to an instrumented airframe, simulating the loads imposed by takeoff, landing and combat manoeuvring at up to 10g. By the summer of 1978, this airframe had clocked up more than 16,000 hours of simulated flight in the rig. These tests were carried out at a careful and deliberate pace which sometimes lagged behind schedule.

As the tests progressed, cracks developed in several structural bulkheads. News of this problem resulted in hostile comments in the media, but GD pointed out in its own defence that the cracks had occurred not in flying aircraft but on ground test specimens. If the risk of such cracks during development testing was not a real one, a company spokesman remarked to the author at the time, no-one would be willing to pay for ground structural test rigs. GD redesigned the affected components, thickening the metal, and installed metal plates to reinforce existing units.

Built up from three major sub-sections – nose/cockpit, centre and aft – the fuselage is based upon conventional frames and longerons. The forward manufacturing break point is just aft of the cockpit, while the second is located forward of the vertical fin.

Combined with advanced aerodynamics and the low sfc of the F100 turbofan, the increase in fuselage internal volume created by wing/body blending accounts for the GD fighter's impressive range performance. Some 28 per cent of the weight of a loaded F-14 is fuel, while the equivalent figure for an F-16 is 31 per cent.

Anyone who has seen an F-16 under-

going an engine change cannot help noticing the effect of wing/body blending on the aircraft's internal fuel capacity. Visiting the Fort Worth flight line in 1977, the author was shown an engineless F-16 – one of the development aircraft on the flight line was undergoing an engine change. Looking up through the tail and out through the air inlet, his first reaction was "Where do you keep the fuel?". At first sight it seemed impossible for so much kerosine to be stowed in the limited space which remained.

Wing/body blending was carried out in three dimensions. Seen from the front or rear of the aircraft, the wing gradually blends in cross section with the fuselage, making it impossible to define where the wing ends and the fuselage begins. This blending is varied lon-

Above: Production aircraft on the Fort Worth assembly line. At this stage the canopy and radome still have protective coverings.

Below: Belgian ground crew prepare an F-16 for flight. The avionics technician needs no steps or ladder in order to work on the radar.

gitudinally in order to 'tailor' the cross-sectional area distribution.

In planform, the wing leading edge also blends with the fuselage thanks to the leading-edge strakes. At high angles of attack, these create vortexes which maintain the energy of the boundary air layer flowing over the inner section of the wing. Wing root stalling is thus delayed, and directional stability maintained. Vortex energy also provides a measure of forebody lift, reducing the need for drag-inducing tail trim. Graphic proof of the existence of these vortexes may be seen during tight turns if local condensation results in a 'con-trail' from the strakes. At air shows, the aircraft has been flown with smoke generators whose plumes have clearly shown the trailing vortexes. And by keeping the inner-wing boundary layer energized, the strakes allowed a reduction in wing size, aspect ratio and weight – a saving of around 500lb (227kg) in structural weight.

The combination of wing/fuselage blending and variable camber resulted in several advantages, including the additional space provided in a location close to the centre of gravity for internal fuel, avionics and other systems. Without this feature, the F-16 would have been about 5ft (1.5m) longer and the structure some 570lb (259kg) heavier.

Gradually increasing thickness of the wing in the region of the wing root resulted in a stiffer wing than would have been possible with a conventional design. Stiffness was increased by the fact that the lift-increasing manoeuvring flaps allowed a smaller wing of reduced span to be used. The wing structure itself incorporates five spars and 11 ribs. Upper and lower wing skins are one-piece machined components.

Aerodynamic performance

Fineness ratio of the F-16 configuration is lower than the ideal for supersonic flight, but transonic drag is minimized. In conventional designs, wing lift normally falls off at high angles of attack, but the F-16 obtains a useful amount of body lift.

The leading-edge manoeuvring flap and trailing-edge flaperon can be moved at up to 35deg/sec to match Mach number and angle of attack. Maximum speed of movement is matched to the aircraft's ability to respond to changes in pitch, so that flaps and aircraft attitude are always matched.

By shaping the wing aerofoil to match aerodynamic conditions, the moving flaps reduce drag, maintain lift at high angles of attack, improve directional stability, and minimize buffeting. The latter qualities are useful during tight turns in air combat, or while 'jinking' at low level to confuse hostile air defences. The wing is only around 1.5in (3.8cm) deep at the point where the

leading-edge rotary actuator is installed, so the design of this component was a significant challenge.

In the spring of 1982 actuator failures caused the USAF temporarily to ground all F-16s which had exceeded 200 hours of operational flying – 240 of the 400 F-16s in service at that time – for inspection of the wing leading-edge flap. A routine inspection had revealed signs of excessive wear in the actuation mechanism which controls the position of the leading-edge manoeuvring flap. More than 40 aircraft required repair, the remainder being returned to service once this component had been inspected – a process which took around five man-hours per aircraft. As an interim solution pending a definitive 'fix', aircraft were re-inspected every 100 hours.

The vertical stabilizer has a multi-spar and multi-rib structure made from aluminium alloy as is the unit's top cap, but the skins are fabricated from graphite epoxy. The two ventral fins beneath the rear fuselage section are made from glass fibre. Also located under the rear fuselage is a runway arrester hook.

The original pattern of horizontal stabilizer is being replaced by a larger component under the MSIP Phase I programme, details of which are given later in this chapter. Inboard of each are the air brakes. Stowed in the horizontal position when not in use, these are of the split type, the upper and lower sections of which open through an angle of 60deg.

The main undercarriage units retract forwards into the lower fuselage, and the large doors were found to offer a good – although unconventional – mounting location for Sparrow or Sky

Above: By early 1979 the production line in GD's mile-long assembly building was picking up speed. The aircraft nearest the camera was delivered to the USAF in May.

Flash radar-guided missiles. The nose gear is located aft of the intake, so that debris or other foreign objects thrown up by the wheel will not be ingested into the engine air intake.

The location of the intake is certainly unconventional, but wind tunnel tests showed that the ventral location is subject to minimal airflow disturbance over a wide range of flight conditions and aircraft manoeuvres, since the forward fuselage tends to shelter it from the effects of aircraft manoeuvres. At an angle of attack of 25deg, for example, the air flows into the intake at an angle of only 10deg.

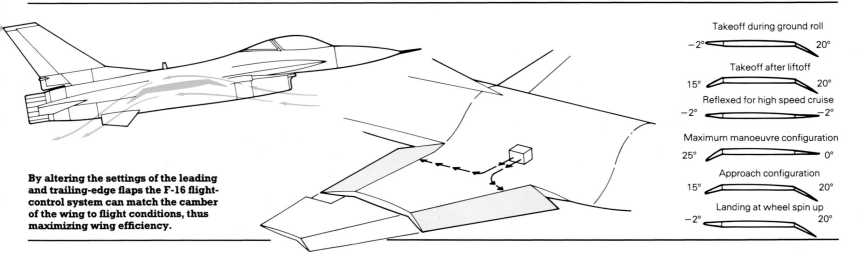

By altering the settings of the leading and trailing-edge flaps the F-16 flight-control system can match the camber of the wing to flight conditions, thus maximizing wing efficiency.

Takeoff during ground roll
−2° / 20°

Takeoff after liftoff
15° / 20°

Reflexed for high speed cruise
−2° / −2°

Maximum manoeuvre configuration
25° / 0°

Approach configuration
15° / 20°

Landing at wheel spin up
−2° / 20°

Critics who predicted in the mid-1970s that the F-16 would suffer a high incidence of engine damage due to FOD (foreign object damage) have been proved wrong. The lower edge of the intake lip is 38in (97.5cm) above the ground, high enough to minimize the chances of small objects or fragments of debris being sucked in. A study of the limited clearance between intake and runway surface on types such as the Boeing 707 (inboard engines) and 737 airliners might have suggested that all would be well, but such obvious comparisons were often overlooked during the wave of F-16 knocking carried out by some 'experts' as Europe was tooling up to build the type.

Conventional wisdom suggests that the complexities of variable geometry are mandatory in an intake for use at Mach 2. Like the creators of the earlier Saab-Scania J37 Viggen, however, the GD engineers ignored the rule book and devised a simple fixed-geometry unit incorporating a boundary-layer splitter plate. This was designed as a single assembly to make future updating easy (a feature later found useful during the development of the turbojet-powered F-16/79 variant). A more traditional variable-geometry intake assembly had been designed, but at present it seems unlikely see service.

In order to reduce the number of spare parts which F-16 units must hold, some components are designed to be interchangeable between port and starboard. These include the horizontal tail surfaces, wing flaperons, 80 per cent of the main landing gear components, and many of the actuator units.

Like any aircraft, the Fighting Falcon is only as good as its pilot. Aircrew assigned to the F-16 are housed in the most sophisticated cockpit that the technology of the early 1970s could devise. Later fighters such as the F/A-18 Hornet may have more advanced electronics, but no other aircraft in the Western world – and probably in the entire world – has the combination of reclining seat and sidestick controller used in the F-16.

Research suggested that a pilot's tolerance could be increased by the use of a reclining seat whose back was tilted at angles of up to 65deg. GD engineers compromised by adopting a tilt of 30deg and by raising the pilot's knees and legs. In terms of providing extra pilot tolerance to high-g manoeuvres the cockpit layout was probably a suc-cess, but the disadvantages of such a configuration seem to have prevented its being used in later designs. Studies carried out by other manufacturers suggest that the raised leg position markedly reduces the panel area which may be used to house displays and instruments.

Good all-round visibility is provided by a canopy whose forward and centre sections are made from a single piece of polycarbonate. An impressive item of plastics engineering, this suffered from 'teething troubles' early in its development. The transparency was required to withstand the impact of a 4lb (1.8kg) bird at 350kt, and passed initial tests with flying colours. Following some minor problems with the canopy protective coating on the YF-16, the USAF modified the latter, but the revised

General Dynamics F-16 Fighting Falcon cutaway

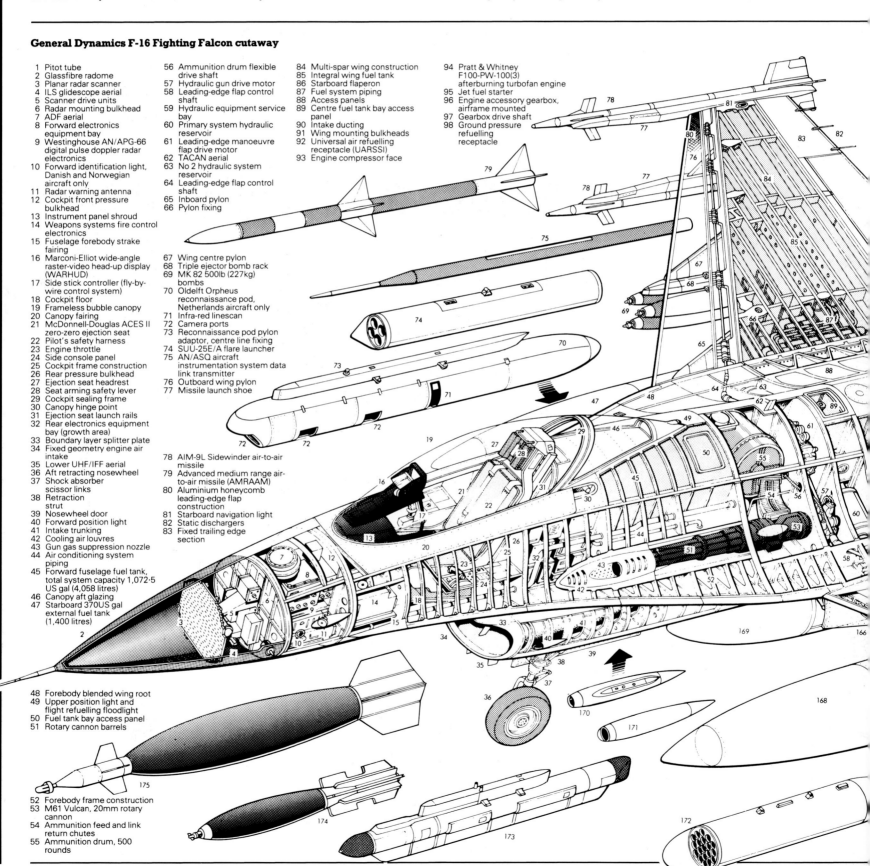

1 Pitot tube
2 Glassfibre radome
3 Planar radar scanner
4 ILS glidescope aerial
5 Scanner drive units
6 Radar mounting bulkhead
7 ADF aerial
8 Forward electronics equipment bay
9 Westinghouse AN/APG-66 digital pulse doppler radar electronics
10 Forward identification light, Danish and Norwegian aircraft only
11 Radar warning antenna
12 Cockpit front pressure bulkhead
13 Instrument panel shroud
14 Weapons systems fire control electronics
15 Fuselage forebody strake fairing
16 Marconi-Elliot wide-angle raster-video head-up display (WARHUD)
17 Side stick controller (fly-by-wire control system)
18 Cockpit floor
19 Frameless bubble canopy
20 Canopy fairing
21 McDonnell-Douglas ACES II zero-zero ejection seat
22 Pilot's safety harness
23 Engine throttle
24 Side console panel
25 Cockpit frame construction
26 Rear pressure bulkhead
27 Ejection seat headrest
28 Seat arming safety lever
29 Cockpit sealing frame
30 Canopy hinge point
31 Ejection seat launch rails
32 Rear electronics equipment bay (growth area)
33 Boundary layer splitter plate
34 Fixed geometry engine air intake
35 Lower UHF/IFF aerial
36 Aft retracting nosewheel
37 Shock absorber scissor links
38 Retraction strut
39 Nosewheel door
40 Forward position light
41 Intake trunking
42 Cooling air louvres
43 Gun gas suppression nozzle
44 Air conditioning system piping
45 Forward fuselage fuel tank, total system capacity 1,072·5 US gal (4,058 litres)
46 Canopy aft glazing
47 Starboard 370US gal external fuel tank (1,400 litres)
48 Forebody blended wing root
49 Upper position light and flight refuelling floodlight
50 Fuel tank bay access panel
51 Rotary cannon barrels
52 Forebody frame construction
53 M61 Vulcan, 20mm rotary cannon
54 Ammunition feed and link return chutes
55 Ammunition drum, 500 rounds
56 Ammunition drum flexible drive shaft
57 Hydraulic gun drive motor
58 Leading-edge flap control shaft
59 Hydraulic equipment service bay
60 Primary system hydraulic reservoir
61 Leading-edge manoeuvre flap drive motor
62 TACAN aerial
63 No 2 hydraulic system reservoir
64 Leading-edge flap control shaft
65 Inboard pylon
66 Pylon fixing
67 Wing centre pylon
68 Triple ejector bomb rack
69 MK 82 500lb (227kg) bombs
70 Oldelft Orpheus reconnaissance pod, Netherlands aircraft only
71 Infra-red linescan
72 Camera ports
73 Reconnaissance pod pylon adaptor, centre line fixing
74 SUU-25E/A flare launcher
75 AN/ASQ aircraft instrumentation system data link transmitter
76 Outboard wing pylon
77 Missile launch shoe
78 AIM-9L Sidewinder air-to-air missile
79 Advanced medium range air-to-air missile (AMRAAM)
80 Aluminium honeycomb leading-edge flap construction
81 Starboard navigation light
82 Static dischargers
83 Fixed trailing edge section
84 Multi-spar wing construction
85 Integral wing fuel tank
86 Starboard flaperon
87 Fuel system piping
88 Access panels
89 Centre fuel tank bay access panel
90 Intake ducting
91 Wing mounting bulkheads
92 Universal air refuelling receptacle (UARSSI)
93 Engine compressor face
94 Pratt & Whitney F100-PW-100(3) afterburning turbofan engine
95 Jet fuel starter
96 Engine accessory gearbox, airframe mounted
97 Gearbox drive shaft
98 Ground pressure refuelling receptacle

design promptly failed its final qualification tests.

This failure triggered off a re-examination of the canopy design and test procedures, and studies of alternative canopy designs. A newer and heavier pattern of canopy was developed in order to ensure adequate resistance to bird strikes. The final design meets all USAF requirements, and offers a level of visibility which must leave MiG-21 and Mirage III pilots drooling with envy. Its high 'bubble' profile may result in some penalty in terms of supersonic drag, but the F100 engine has more than enough thrust to cope. Visibility from the cockpit covers a full 360deg in the horizontal plane, and from 15deg down over the nose through the zenith and back to directly behind – a total of 195 deg. Sideways visibility extends down

Above: A technician examines the forward undercarriage leg of a Belgian Air Force F-16. Note the inlet strut for increased rigidity

to a depression angle of 40deg. The polycarbonate is 0.5in (1.3cm) thick, but its optical quality is high, and the curved surfaces offer minimal distortion of the outside view.

The ejection seat selected for production F-16s was the McDonnell Douglas ACES II (Advanced Concept Ejection Seat) used on the F-15 Eagle. This is a rocket-powered unit with a vectored-thrust STAPAC pitch-control system. Mounted beneath the seat, STAPAC consists of a small vernier rocket motor with a thrust of 235lb (107kg) and a 0.3sec burn time. As the seat leaves the cockpit, a gas generator spins up a pitch-rate gyro. This is uncaged and the vernier motor lit. The latter normally has its thrust axis aligned with the nominal centre of gravity of the seat and its occupant: should the seat pitch forwards

or backwards due to aerodynamic forces or a low or high centre of gravity, the STAPAC vernier will be vectored to apply a corrective force.

ACES II offers zero-zero performance. From a stationary aircraft parked on the ground, it will lift to a height of more than 100ft (30m) and carry rearwards by at least 50ft (15m). Built-in survival equipment includes emergency oxygen, a URT-33C radio beacon, a liferaft and a rucksack.

The Multinational Staged Improvement Plan (MSIP) approved in February 1981 brought in a series of improvements developed under Engineering Change Proposal ECP350. This included modifications to the structure and wiring of the wings to allow the carriage of AMRAAM, the provision of hardpoints on the intake sides to carry

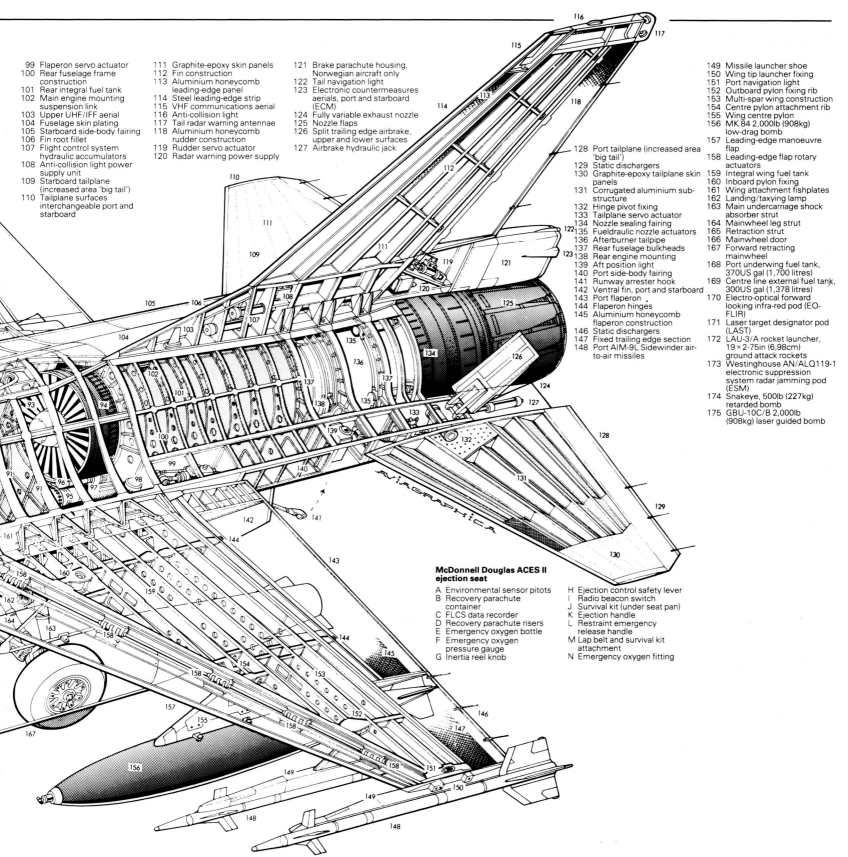

99 Flaperon servo actuator
100 Rear fuselage frame construction
101 Rear integral fuel tank
102 Main engine mounting suspension link
103 Upper UHF/IFF aerial
104 Fuselage skin plating
105 Starboard side-body fairing
106 Fin root fillet
107 Flight control system hydraulic accumulators
108 Anti-collision light power supply unit
109 Starboard tailplane (increased area 'big tail')
110 Tailplane surfaces interchangeable port and starboard

111 Graphite-epoxy skin panels
112 Fin construction
113 Aluminium honeycomb leading-edge panel
114 Steel leading-edge strip
115 VHF communications aerial
116 Anti-collision light
117 Tail radar warning antennae
118 Aluminium honeycomb rudder construction
119 Rudder servo actuator
120 Radar warning power supply

121 Brake parachute housing, Norwegian aircraft only
122 Tail navigation light
123 Electronic countermeasures aerials, port and starboard (ECM)
124 Fully variable exhaust nozzle
125 Nozzle flaps
126 Split trailing edge airbrake, upper and lower surfaces
127 Airbrake hydraulic jack

128 Port tailplane (increased area 'big tail')
129 Static dischargers
130 Graphite-epoxy tailplane skin panels
131 Corrugated aluminium substructure
132 Hinge pivot fixing
133 Tailplane servo actuator
134 Nozzle sealing fairing
135 Fueldraulic nozzle actuators
136 Afterburner tailpipe
137 Rear fuselage bulkheads
138 Rear engine mounting
139 Aft position light
140 Port side-body fairing
141 Runway arrester hook
142 Ventral fin, port and starboard
143 Port flaperon
144 Flaperon hinges
145 Aluminium honeycomb flaperon construction
146 Static dischargers
147 Fixed trailing edge section
148 Port AIM-9L Sidewinder air-to-air missiles

149 Missile launcher shoe
150 Wing tip launcher fixing
151 Port navigation light
152 Outboard pylon fixing rib
153 Multi-spar wing construction
154 Centre pylon attachment rib
155 Wing centre pylon
156 MK 84 2,000lb (908kg) low-drag bomb
157 Leading-edge manoeuvre flap
158 Leading-edge flap rotary actuators
159 Integral wing fuel tank
160 Inboard pylon fixing
161 Wing attachment fishplates
162 Landing/taxiing lamp
163 Main undercarriage shock absorber strut
164 Mainwheel leg strut
165 Retraction strut
166 Mainwheel door
167 Forward retracting mainwheel
168 Port underwing fuel tank, 370US gal (1,700 litres)
169 Centre line external fuel tank, 300US gal (1,378 litres)
170 Electro-optical forward looking infra-red pod (EO-FLIR)
171 Laser target designator pod (LAST)
172 LAU-3/A rocket launcher, 19 × 2·75in (6,98cm) ground attack rockets
173 Westinghouse AN/ALQ119-1 electronic suppression system radar jamming pod (ESM)
174 Snakeye, 500lb (227kg) retarded bomb
175 GBU-10C/B 2,000lb (908kg) laser guided bomb

McDonnell Douglas ACES II ejection seat

A Environmental sensor pitots
B Recovery parachute container
C FLCS data recorder
D Recovery parachute risers
E Emergency oxygen bottle
F Emergency oxygen pressure gauge
G Inertia reel knob

H Ejection control safety lever
I Radio beacon switch
J Survival kit (under seat pan)
K Ejection handle
L Restraint emergency release handle
M Lap belt and survival kit attachment
N Emergency oxygen fitting

the LANTIRN electro-optical system, and wiring and structural provisions in the cockpit for the LANTIRN HUD, head-down multi-function displays and other improved avionics.

Load capacity of the centre wing pylons rises from 2,500lb (1,135kg) to 3,500lb (1,590kg). Other modifications prepare the aircraft for the ASPJ ECM system and make provision for a radar altimeter. Control logic of the aircraft environmental control system was also modified to increase system efficiency.

MSIP I modifications

Although the USAF does not expect to take delivery of the new avionics items until the end of 1984, it programmed the associated structural and wiring modifications into the production line in 1981 under the MSIP I programme. These changes added approximately 200lb (90kg) to aircraft weight.

A new horizontal tailplane of increased area is the most obvious external evidence of the MSIP I modifications. Introduced by Engineering Change Proposal 425, this provides the greater control force required to cope with heavy munition loads. When large ordnance loads are carried, aircraft centre of gravity is moved further forward, increasing stability and making the F-16 more difficult to manoeuvre.

The revised tail is easier and less expensive to produce, since its structure does not incorporate titanium. The rising cost and poor availability of this metal led GD to redesign the tailplane spar and pivot in aluminium as part of ECP 425, resulting in a cost saving of 20 per cent. Corrugated aluminium alloy, mechanically fastened to the carbon-fibre skins, replaced the earlier filling of aluminium honeycomb, which was bonded into place. The finished

stabilizer is thicker than the original component, but thanks to the increased span the thickness-to-chord ratio remains unchanged. At the same time, the need for a braking parachute led GD to modify the vertical fin to allow the fitting of this item should customers so desire.

Wherever possible, the design makes maintenance easy. Ground crew working on the F-4 Phantom had to cope with 510 individual lubrication points, 281 fuel line connections, more than 900 individual electrical connectors and 294 avionics units. In the case of Fighting Falcon, lubrication points have been cut to 84, and fuel line connections to 90, while the avionics technicians have only 52 units to deal with. The number of connectors remains high at 841, but these now incorporate silicone grommets, so are easier to service than earlier patterns of connector which were potted (sealed) with rubberized compound after assembly. As a further aid to maintenance, around 60 per cent of the surface of the aircraft is removable, the Fighting Falcon design incorporating 228 access doors. Only four tools are required to open these, and 80 per cent of the aircraft systems are accessible without stands.

Old technology

Some technology from earlier General Dynamics fighters – the Convair F-102 Delta Dagger and F-106 Delta Dart – was used in the F-16 programme. Tests have shown that a fuel tank sealant designated AF-10 Scotchweld which was used on these 1950s designs had a better performance and required less maintenance than the more modern polysulphide rubber-like compounds now in use, and offered cost savings of 25 per cent or more. During tests on F-16 centre-fuselage and aft-fuselage

tanks, the older type of sealant successfully withstood the standard 5psi (0.35kg/sq cm) air-pressure test.

The most drastic structural modification which the Fighting Falcon has undergone was that imposed by the 'cranked-wing' F-16XL project, whose new delta wing uses a planform originally proposed for use on supersonic airliners. Developed in conjunction with NASA's Langley Research Centre, it is intended to offer low drag at high subsonic and supersonic speeds without losing low-speed manoeuvrability. It is of multispar delta design with a leading edge sweep angle varying from 50deg to 70deg. Area is 120 per cent greater than that of the basic wing, while wing weight rises by 2,600lb (1,179kg). Weight is reduced by the use of carbon

composite materials for the upper and lower skins. Had these been made of aluminium alloy, the wing would have been some 600lb (272kg) heavier.

During the conversion work, the length of the aircraft fuselage was extended by 56in (142cm) This was accomplished by adding two new fuselage sections at the junctions between the three main fuselage sub-assemblies. One 30in (76cm) section is located at the front split point, and a 26in (66cm) section at the rear. This increase in fuselage and wing size allowed internal fuel capacity to be increased by 82 per cent. The latter factor dramatically increases the payload/range performance of the modified aircraft. The F-16XL is intended to carry twice the payload of the F-16 40 per cent further.

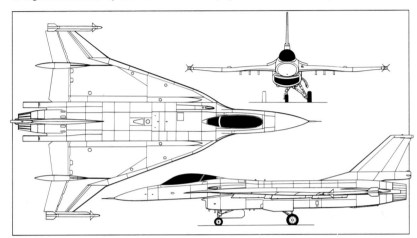

Above: Single-seat version of the F-16XL

Below: The modular design of the basic F-16 fuselage allowed new sections to be spliced in to create the longer fuselage of the F-16XL.

Below right: The first F-16XL was a single-seat aircraft powered by a P&W F100 turbofan and with a wing area increased by 120 per cent.

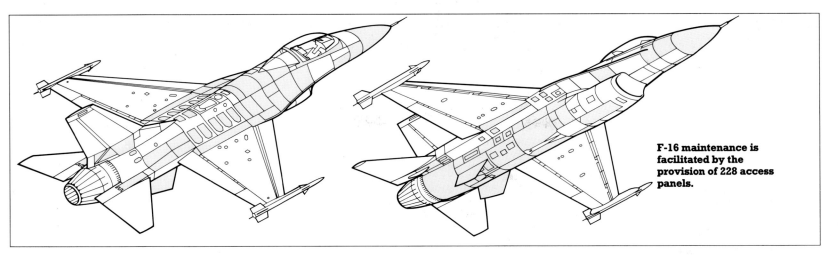

F-16 maintenance is facilitated by the provision of 228 access panels.

Above: A USAF technician removes an access panel from the wing of a 428th Tactical Fighter Squadron F-16 during Exercise Cope Elite 1981.

Right: Although the wing planforms of the F-16/79 (lower) and F-16XL are very different, the fuselage displays a high degree of commonality.

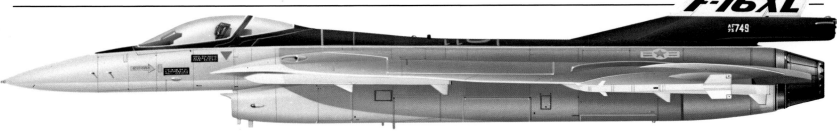

F-16 Fighting Falcon detail comparisons

1. Nose section of the F-16B and D trainers.
2. F-16/AFTI with intake-mounted canards, and dorsal spine containing avionics and instrumentation.
3. Plan view of F-16A and C single-seat versions.
4. Single-seat F-16XL with cranked arrow wing.
5. Tailplane fitted to early production aircraft.
6. Definitive tailplane of increased area.
7. Rear fuselage of F-16/79.
8. Norwegian aircraft have a modified tail fairing which houses a braking parachute.

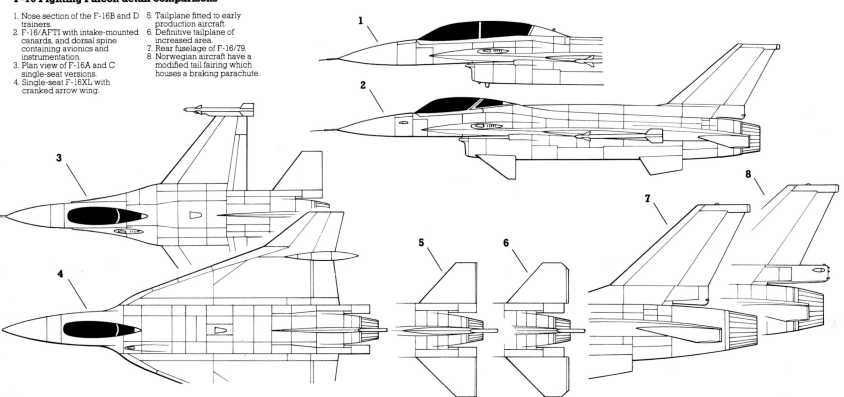

Powerplant

John Boyd's concept of Specific Excess Power called for the F-16 to have a high thrust-to-weight ratio, which in turn required an engine of superlative performance. Such a powerplant was already available in the form of the F100 turbofan devised by Pratt & Whitney for the earlier F-15 Eagle programme. The F100 could deliver the thrust, but its development and deployment stretched US engine technology to the limits. Despite a series of teething troubles, however, the USAF and P&W persisted with development work until all problems were solved.

Development of the Pratt & Whitney F100 turbofan started in August 1968, when the USAF awarded development contracts to P & W and General Electric for engines suitable for use in the planned FX fighter – later to become the F-15 Eagle. In view of the high thrust-to-weight ratio planned for the new fighter, the resulting engines would have to push the technology of the time to its limits. P&W faced the daunting task of developing a powerplant producing 25 per cent more thrust per pound of weight than the contemporary TF30 turbofan used in the F-111, and twice that of the J75 turbojet used in the F-105 Thunderchief and F-106 Delta Dart.

Both companies built and ran demonstration engines whose light weight, high thrust and low fuel consumption put them well ahead of previous designs. The P&W engine was selected by the USAF for further development, contracts being awarded in 1970. Two versions were originally planned – the F100 for the USAF and the F401 intended to power later models of the US Navy's F-14 Tomcat, though the latter was cancelled when the USN was ordered by the Department of Defense to cut back the size of the planned F-14 fleet.

The F100 is an axial-flow turbofan with a bypass ratio of 0.7:1. It has two shafts, one carrying a three-stage fan driven by a two-stage turbine, the other carrying the ten-stage main compressor and its two-stage turbine. The completed engine is 191in (4.85m) long and, 34.8in (0.88m) in diameter at the inlet, and weighs 3,068lb (1,392kg).

New technologies used in the F100 included powder metallurgy. Instead of forming some metal components in the traditional manner, P&W reduced the raw material to a powder. This could be heated and formed under high pressure to create engine components better able to tolerate the high temperatures planned for the F100 core.

Operating temperature of the F100 turbine was far above that of earlier engines. Successful turbojets of earlier vintage, such as the GE F85 which powers the F-5E, or the GE J79 used in the F-4 and F-104, had turbine inlet temperatures of around 1,800deg F (982 deg C). P&W had achieved figures of just over 2,000deg F (1,093deg C) in the TF30 turbofan, but to meet the demanding requirements of the F100 specification involved temperatures of 2,565deg F (1,407deg C).

Use of such advanced technology resulted in an engine capable of providing the high levels of thrust required by the F-15 and F-16. Maximum thrust is normally described as being 'in the 15,000lb (6,800kg) thrust class' when running without afterburner, and 'in the 25,000lb (11,340kg) class' at full augmentation.

Normal dry (non-afterburning) rating is 12,420lb (5,634kg), rising to a maximum of 14,670lb (6,654kg) at full Military Intermediate rating – the maximum attainable without afterburning. Specific fuel consumption (sfc) – the amount of thrust produced for each pound of fuel burned per hour – is 0.69 at normal rating, 0.71 at Military Intermediate. At full afterburning power, the F100 develops 23,830lb (10,809kg) of thrust at an sfc of 2.17. At this rating, the engine swallows an impressive 860lb (390kg) of fuel per minute.

By the time the F-15 Eagle was ready for its first flight in July 1972, the F100 had completed most of its test programme, meeting 23 out of 24 critical 'project milestones'. Between February and October of the following year, a series of turbine failures dogged attempts to complete the 150-hour running trial which formed part of the formal Qualification Test. The latter was the most punishing series of tests to which any US military jet engine had ever been subjected, according to P&W. It included 30 hours of running at a simulated speed of mach 2.3, and 38 hours of running at a simulated Mach 1.6.

Following completion of this test, the F100 was subjected to a further series of intensive trials, including 150 hours of running at over-temperature conditions, and a long series of Accelerated Mission Tests. Conducted on the ground, but designed to simulate the stresses of operational service, these were intended to build up running time and detect potential problems. None of these was serious enough to delay the start of F-15 production, and the first

Above: A USAF crewman at Kunsan Air Base in South Korea fuels an F-16. Engines in the F100 thrust class require large amounts of fuel.

Below: At full afterburning thrust, the F100 consumes more than 800lb of fuel per minute. This aircraft is from the 8th TFW, based at Kunsan.

aircraft were delivered to the USAF in November 1974. The F-15 powerplant is designated F100-PW-100 by the company and JTF22A-25A by the USAF.

Despite the obvious merits of the P&W F100 turbofan, including the fact that this engine had already been selected for use on the F-15, GD carried out many studies of the smaller General Electric YF101 engine. The P&W engine was very much a product of late 1960s thinking – a high bypass ratio turbofan offering good and economical performance at its military (dry) rating – while the GE powerplant was a more modern engine with a much lower bypass ratio. Only a small amount of air was ducted past the core in this design, which GE had dubbed a 'leaky turbojet'.

In many ways, the GE engine was more conservatively designed, emphasis having been placed on reliability rather than ultimate performance. GE personnel made no secret of their view that the P&W engine was pushing the technology of the time close to the limits.

Factors considered by GD during the engine evaluation were the weight of the rival powerplants plus the fuel needed for cruise, combat and reserve. The YF-16 design mission included a 500nm cruise to the target area at high subsonic speed, acceleration to combat speed using maximum afterburner, a period of combat in full afterburner involving sustained turns and supersonic and subsonic speeds, then a return to base with a 20-minute sea-level reserve.

Weight calculations

Combined fuel and engine weight for this mission was calculated to be 7,882lb (3,575kg) using a single F100, or 10,234lb (4,642kg) for twin YF101 engines. Two YF101 engines plus installation would weigh 1,024lb (464kg) more than would be the case with a single F100, while an extra 1,328lb (602kg) of fuel would have to be carried. Using the twin GE installation, the F-16 design team would have come up with an aircraft with a mission weight of 21,470lb (9,739kg) instead of the 17,050lb (7,734kg) promised by the P&W engine.

If aircraft weight were kept constant, an F100-engined YF-16 would have a 70 per cent greater mission radius than a twin-YF101 design. GD estimated. Some 90 per cent of this increase was due in roughly equal proportions to the lower engine weight and fuel load required by an F100-powered design, the remainder to reduced drag and airframe weight.

The lower bypass ratio and lighter weight of the F100 installation produced dividends in many areas, GD estimated. Under static conditions at sea level, a pair of YF101 'leaky turbojets' would produce an extra 5,200lb (2,359kg) of thrust, but at Mach 1.2 the turbofan

offered an additional 7,500lb (3,402kg). The difference at 30,000ft (9,000m) and Mach 2 was less marked, but the P&W engine still offered a useful 2,850lb (1,293kg) of extra thrust.

In cruising flight, the big turbofan offered a thrust-to-weight ratio seven per cent better than that of the two YF101 engines, and with a 25 per cent lower fuel flow. At 30,000ft and Mach 2, fuel flow was more evenly matched, but thrust-to-weight ratio was dramatically improved. The P&W engine would consume 6.5 per cent less fuel, but produce a 41 per cent higher thrust-to-weight ratio.

In one instance the F100 turned out to have too much thrust. The residual thrust from an idling F100 was 670lb (304kg) – too high for F-16 operations on icy runways. In theory, this residual thrust could have sent a lightly-loaded

F-16 moving at speeds of up to 50kt, rather too much for taxiing. A test programme using the second YF-16 showed that the engine could be adjusted to give a lower idling speed, reducing the taxiing speed to a more acceptable figure.

USAF hopes that the F100 would be a mature powerplant by the time the F-16 entered service were dimmed by a series of technical and operational problems. Strikes at two major subcontractors delayed the delivery of engines, while service experience showed that the F100 was wearing out twice as fast as had been predicted. By the end of 1979 the USAF was being forced to accept engineless F-15 airframes, and by the spring of the following year some 30 were in storage. A massive effort by P&W brought the delivery situation under control, but for

Above: To clear the F100 for service, the engine was subjected to the most demanding series of ground tests ever devised for a USAF powerplant.

a long time the F-15 and F-16 fleets remained short of engines.

A modification introduced into the fuel pump of the F100 created problems for the F-15 early in that aircraft's career. In cruising flight, cavitation could begin in the pump, badly damaging the pump vanes. The solution adopted on the F-15 was simple – revert to the original design. In the case of the F-16, a pump failure would be more serious, so Sundstrand developed an

Below: Specifically developed for use in the F-16, the F100-PW-200 has additional anti-stagnation-stall features for single-engine safety.

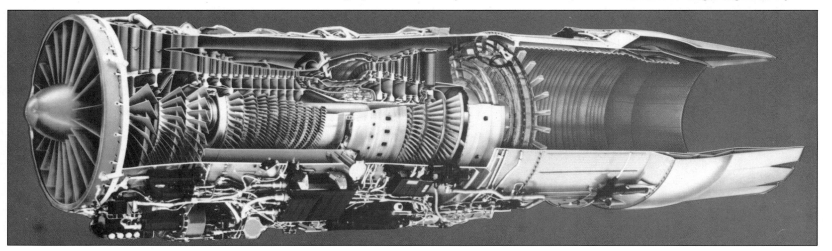

alternative dual-element pump for this aircraft. This runs at a lower speed, and should one section fail, the other can continue to deliver fuel at a lower rate.

The electronic engine control unit uses the fuel as a coolant. This technique for obtaining 'free' cooling led to problems when the F-15 first entered service. During training missions at Luke AFB, aircraft sometimes had to wait for 45 minutes or more before takeoff, with engines running at idle settings. This gradually heated the mass of fuel in the Eagle's tank to the point where it was no longer cold enough to cool the engine control unit. Given the high temperature of the desert environment at Luke, the unit could not radiate the excess heat away, so tended to overheat, resulting in engine overspeed problems and turbine failures.

Early operational and durability problems with the F100 during the late 1970s were largely overcome by modifications, plus improvements in materials, maintenance and operating procedures. Production of spare parts was accelerated, and field maintenance teams were increased in size.

Part of the problem lay in the fact that the USAF had underestimated the number of cycles which engines aboard such high-performance types as the F-15 and F-16 would actually undergo. (A cycle is defined as the temperature variation experienced in a mission from engine start to maximum power and afterburner, then back to the lower settings used for landing.) In 1977 the service estimated that each engine would undergo 1.15 cycles per flight hour, but in practice the rate was 2.2 for the F-15 and 3.1 for the F-16.

At one time, designers had assumed that the most arduous duty which a jet engine had to face was running for long periods at high power levels. By the late 1960s, research had shown that this was simply not the case. Many failures were due to this type of running, but others were created by the heating and cooling resulting from an engine being run up to high power then throttled back.

Technicians dubbed this 'low-cycle fatigue', but had to admit that it was difficult to measure. To aid the design of future engines such as the F100, estimates were made of the average number of thermal cycles to which an engine would be exposed per flying

hour. Unfortunately for the F100 programme, these estimates were wrong. In practice, engines were being subjected to far more thermal cycles than the designers had allowed for.

Paradoxically, the additional stress which the engines were receiving was largely due to the F-15 and F-16 being such good aircraft. Given the high manoeuvrability of their new mounts, pilots were flying in a manner not possible on earlier types, pushing the aircraft to high angles of attack and making full use of the extended performance envelope. In the heat of a dogfight, the throttle setting would be changed much more often than on earlier fighters. All this spelled hard work for the engine.

Air combat demands

The F-16 places more strain on the engine than does the F-15, since the Fighting Falcon is used in the demanding air-combat role. P&W studies showed that throttle excursions placed a greater strain on the engine than long runs at a constant setting. Studies involving instrumented test aircraft gathered data on the number of throttle movements and the amount of afterburner use which test F-16s were clocking up, and the company carried out a series of accelerated mission tests to clear the F100 for use in the GD aircraft.

Critical components such as first-stage turbine blades showed signs of distress, condemnation rate during repair being 60 per cent instead of the predicted 20 per cent. Maximum gas temperature was reduced to conserve component life, while R&D funding was concentrated on improvements to reliability rather than increasing thrust. Despite these problems, the F-15 had a better engine-related safety record by the end of the 1970s than any other USAF fighter at a comparable point in its service career.

Another problem which was to dog the F100 during the first years of its service career was stagnation stalling. The compressor blades in a jet engine are of aerofoil section, and, like the wing of an aircraft, can be stalled if the angle at which the airflow strikes them exceeds a critical value. Powerplant stalls are occasional occurrences in most jet engines, particularly in the early stages of development, but the F100 was to prove excessively vulner-

able to stagnation stalling during its first few years of operational service.

Turbofans are prone to a particularly severe type of stall from which recovery is not possible. As the flow of air through the compressor is disturbed, the engine core looses speed, while the combustor section of the engine continues to pass hot gas to the turbine, causing the latter to overheat. If this condition is not noticed, the turbine may be damaged.

Experience with the F-15 showed that in the event of a mild hard start, the pilot might not notice that a stall had occurred, as the loss of acceleration on the twin-engined aircraft was often not sharp enough to indicate to the pilot that one engine had failed. Without a check on the temperature gauge, low-pressure turbine entry temperature could reach the point where damage might occur. To avoid this problem, an audible-warning system was devised for the Eagle. This is not needed on the Fighting Falcon, since a stall of the single engine produces an immediate loss of acceleration.

Some stagnation stalls were found to be due to component failures, but most were linked with afterburner problems. The latter usually took the form of 'hard starts' – virtually mini-explosions within the afterburner. In some cases the afterburner failed to light on schedule; in other instances the burner extinguished. In either event, large amounts of unburned fuel were sprayed into the jetpipe, creating a momentary build-up of fuel. When this was ignited by the hot efflux from the engine core, a pressure pulse was created – the aerospace equivalent of a car backfiring.

Deliberate hard start

A reporter from *Aviation Week* gave this account of a deliberately induced hard start on a test stand: "The force of the auto-ignition was sufficient to rock the heavily sound-insulated concrete test building. A large gout of flame at the afterburner exhaust was seen on the closed-circuit colour-television system." The pressure in the afterburner resulting from a hard start sent a shock wave back up through the fan duct. When this reached the front section of the engine, it could cause the fan to stall, the high-pressure compressor to stall, or, in the worst case, both. It was sometimes possible for a series of stagnation stalls

Above: Dwarfed by the bulk of the McDonnell Douglas KC-10A Extender, an F-16 connects the 'flying boom' to its receptacle during tests of the new tanker/cargo aircraft.

to occur, with each resulting in the afterburner hard start needed to trigger off another.

Stagnation stalls usually took place at altitude and at high Mach numbers, but rarely below 20,000ft (6,100m). Normal recovery method was for the pilot to shut down the engine and allow it to spool down. Once the tachometer showed that engine rpm had fallen below the 50 per cent mark, the throttle could safely be reopened to the idle position, and the F100 would carry out its automatic relight sequence. The F-16 is fitted with a jet-fuel starter, but from a height of 35,000ft (10,700m) a pilot would probably have enough time to attempt at least three unassisted starts using ram air. Critical factor in restarting the engine after a stagnation stall is the low-pressure turbine-inlet temperature. This must fall to 450deg F (232deg C) before the engine can be restarted.

Several modifications were devised to reduce the frequency of stagnation stalls. The first approach taken was to try to prevent pressure build-ups in the afterburner. A quartz window in the side of the afterburner assembly allowed a flame sensor to monitor the pilot flame of the augmentor. If this went out, the flow of fuel to the outer sections of the burner was prevented.

When the F100 engine-control system was originally designed, P&W engineers allowed for the possibility that ingestion of efflux from missiles might stall the engine and a 'rocket fire' facility was designed into the controls. When missiles were fired, an electronic signal could be sent to the unified fuel control system which supplies fuel to the engine core and to the afterburner. The angle of the variable stator blades in the engine could be altered to avoid a stall, while the fuel flow to the engine was momentarily reduced, and the afterburner exhaust was increased in area to reduce the magnitude of any pressure pulse in the afterburner.

Tests had shown that the 'rocket fire' facility was not needed, but P&W engineers were able to use it as a means of preventing stagnation stalls. Engine

Above: A night-time engine test at the Pratt & Whitney plant. The F100 is in full afterburner, and the nozzle has been fully opened to allow the hot exhaust gases to expand.

shaft speed, turbine temperature and the angle of the compressor stator blades are monitored on the F100 by a digital electronic engine control unit, which normally serves to 'fine-tune' the engine throughout flight to ensure optimum performance.

By monitoring and comparing HP spool speed and fan exhaust temperature, the engine control unit is able to sense that a stagnation stall is about to take place, and send a dummy 'Rocket Fire' signal to the unified fuel control system to initiate the anti-stall measures described above. At the same time, a second modification to the fuel control system reduces the afterburner setting to zone 1 – little more than a pilot light – in order to help reduce pressure within the jetpipe.

In an attempt to prevent any pulses coming forward through the fan duct from affecting the core, P&W engineers devised a modification known as the 'proximate splitter'. This is a forward extension to the internal casing which splits the incoming airflow from the engine compressor fan, passing some to the core of the engine and diverting the remainder down the fan duct, past the core and into the afterburner. By closing the gap between the front end of this casing and the rear of the fan to just under half an inch, the engine designers reduced the size of the path by which the high-pressure pulses from the burner had been reaching the core. Engines fitted with the proximate splitter were test-flown in the F-15, but this modification was not embodied in the engines of production Eagles, whose twin engines made the loss of a single engine less hazardous.

When it first flew, the F-16 seemed almost free of stagnation stall problems, but while flying with an early-model F100 engine, one of the YF-16 prototypes did experience a stagnation stall,

Right: Ready for refuelling during a 4,350 mile (7,000km) flight across the United States intended to simulate a transatlantic deployment, an F-16 approaches the boom of a KC-135.

though this occurred outside the normal performance envelope. Three incidents were noted later during flight tests at high angles of attack. All took place at Edwards AFB during low-speed flight tests at high altitude. The first production aircraft to experience a stagnation stall was an FAéB aircraft operating near the limits of the performance envelope. The pilot was able to restart the engine and landed safely.

Given the amount of development work, the stagnation stall problem was soon mastered, although never completely eliminated. To suit the F100 for the single-engined F-16, the USAF decided to adopt the modifications already fitted to the engines of the F-15, plus the proximate splitter.

The F-16 powerplant is designated F100-PW-200 by the manufacturer, JTF22A-33 by the USAF. It weighs 54lb (24.5kg) more than the original version fitted to the F-15, and incorporates a back-up fuel-control system and a modified cooling system for the control system, which has a hydromechanical back-up.

The improvement in reliability was dramatic. Back in 1976, the F-15 fleet experienced a stagnation stall rate of 11–12 per 1,000 flying hours. By the end of 1981 this had dropped to 1.5 per 1,000 hours thanks to the modifications to the fuel control system and nozzle. Engines fitted to the F-16 fleet (and incorporating the proximate splitter) had an even lower rate – 0.15 per 1,000 hours.

The need for greater engine reliability in the single-seat F-16 has forced the USAF to be cautious when problems emerge. In the summer of 1980, for example, engines in USAF, European and Israeli service were inspected following the discovery of a broken control cable in the wreckage of an aircraft which crashed at Hill AFB during a low-level training flight. This was seen as a precautionary measure for the single-seat aircraft: for the twin-engined F-15 spot checks were deemed sufficient.

Efforts are under way to reduce further the smoke output of the F100 as part of a planned component-improvement programme. For example, the combustor has been modified to increase the velocity of the airflow in its front end. This results in improved mixing of air and fuel and leads to more complete combustion and less residual smoke.

Traditional engine-servicing techniques involve replacing critical components at the end of a statistically calculated lifetime. This often results in components being removed and scrap-

Below: A pilot of the 429th Tactical Fighter Wing carries out a pre-flight inspection of his Fighting Falcon's ventral intake.

ped while still perfectly serviceable, giving good safety margins, but at a high cost to the operator. The USAF now wants engine designers to develop parts with greater tolerance to crack damage so that these may be left in the engine until inspection by non-destructive test (NDT) methods shows that cracks are starting to develop and a replacement is needed. Life-cycle costs may be cut by up to 60 per cent.

The service's Damage Tolerant Design (DTD) programme involved both Pratt & Whitney and General Electric, and focussed much of its attention on the F100. One of the programme's first achievements was a new pattern of F100 fan disc having five times the life of the original component. Key design elements under DTD are high quality control of the raw material, and the avoidance of shapes and configurations which cause stress concentrations – sharp radii, for example.

New components
The USAF plans to begin testing engine discs currently under development as part of the DTD programme in 1984, and hopes to fit these into operational engines before the end of that year. By 1985 or 1986 the F100 may be fitted with second and third-stage turbine blades and vanes manufactured using a single-crystal technique. Although more expensive than components made from traditional materials, these will probably have a lifetime at least twice that of current vanes and blades.

The USAF was the first F100 user to take advantage of a warranty scheme offered by P&W in 1980, whereby the company undertook to repair or replace certain high-pressure turbines unserviceable as a result of wear or mechanical failure at no extra cost to the USAF. Engines covered by the deal were from production lot IX and were due for delivery between February 1981 and January 1982.

To qualify for free treatment, faulty engines would have to have carried out less than 900 equivalents of the TAC engine operating cycle (about two years of normal use) or have developed the fault within three and a half years of delivery. If the HP failure had caused secondary damage to the engine, P&W undertook to cover costs up to 75 per cent of that of a new engine.

An "engine war"
In its search for an alternative engine for the F-16 and the US Navy's F-14 Tomcat, the US Department of Defense awarded General Electric a $79.7 million contract to build a small batch of 27,000lb (12,250kg) thrust F101 Derivative Fighter Engines (F101DFE) for flight test.

The new powerplant was based on the F101 used in the B-1 bomber, but incor-

porated components derived from the F404 engine used on the F/A-18 Hornet. These included a scaled-up fan, modified afterburner and nozzle. Flight tests started in December 1981 using an F-16, followed by US Navy tests in an F-14 Tomcat.

Both services were impressed. The Navy adopted the engine as a replacement for Tomcat's current P&W TF30 while the USAF began what the US aerospace industry soon dubbed "the Great Engine War" by announcing its intention to split future fighter engine purchases between Pratt & Whitney and General Electric. GE was given a $109.3 million contract for full-scale development of the new engine, which would be known as the F110.

Similar in overall dimensions to the F100, the F110 is 181in (460cm) in length, 46.5in (118cm) in diameter, and weighs 3,830lb (1,737kg). A three-stage fan leads to a nine-stage compressor, the first three stages of which are variable. Bypass ratio is 0.87.

The annular combustion chamber is designed for smokeless operation, and has 20 dual-cone fuel injectors and swirl-cup vaporizers. The single-stage HP turbine is designed to cope with a turbine inlet temperature of approximately 2,500 degrees F (1,370 C). Blades are individually replaceable without rotor disassembly. An uncooled two-stage LP turbine leads to the fully-modulated afterburner. When afterburning is demanded, fuel is injected into both the fan and core flows, which mix prior to combustion.

Throughout the battle between the two powerplants, the USAF has stayed neutral, with the share in orders being split close to 50:50. All F110s ordered by the USAF are for use on the F-16; the F100 remains the standard F-15 powerplant. Between the start of the "engine war" in 1984 and the early 1990s, around 75 per cent of the F-16s bought by the USAF were GE-powered.

The advantages of having a single engine able to fit both the F-15 and F-16 was obvious, so P&W developed the current F100-PW-220 model. A link in one of the electrical connectors which mates to the engine allows the engine control system to determine the type of aircraft to which it has been fitted. It can then automatically match the engine to the airframe, ensuring that (for example) fuel flows match the inlet type and current inlet airflow condition.

By the end of 1990 the -220 had clocked up more than 300,000 flight hours with the air forces of ten nations. Identical in thrust to the existing -100 and -200, it has proved a reliable powerplant, eclipsing the performance of the earlier -200. The number of engines needing maintenance shop work had fallen by 65 per cent, while the unscheduled shutdown rate was down by 85 per cent. By the end of 1990, no F100-PW-220-powered aircraft has suffered an engine-caused Class A accident (a category which usually results in an airframe write-off). Older engines can be rebuilt to the -220E standard, becoming directly interchangeable with the new-build -220 model. The USAF has embarked on the reworking of around 3,000 existing engines, and the -220E retrofit has also been adopted by Israel, Pakistan and Saudi Arabia.

The -220 will remain in production for export probably to beyond the year 2000, but by the winter of 1991/92 the USAF had switched to the new F100-PW-229 rated at 29,100lb (13,199kg) with full afterburner. This has a higher fan airflow and pressure ratio, a higher-airflow compressor with an extra stage, a new float-wall combustor, higher turbine temperatures, and a redesigned afterburner.

Sea-level bench ratings give the newer engine offers around 22 per cent more thrust than the older models. In practice, the increase can be up to 35 per cent, depending on flight conditions, says P&W. In clean conditions, -229 powered F-15s and F-16s have flown supersonically on dry thrust.

F100-PW-229 engines were test-flown in the F-15A, F-15E, F-16B, and F-16C. First deliveries took place in December 1989, but these engines were not fitted to production aircraft. Instead they were earmarked for USAF Operational Capability Release (OCR) and Field Service Evaluation (FSE) trials intended to wring any remaining bugs out of the uprated powerplant. It was a wise move; in the summer of 1991, the engine was briefly grounded following the discovery of manufacturing flaws in diffuser cases.

Production deliveries of F-15s fitted with the new engine began in late 1991, with the first F-16s following in 1992. Existing Block 30/32 and 40/42 aircraft will not be re-engined. At a time of shrinking defence budgets, these aircraft will retain the -220 and -220E.

The degree of mechanical change in the -229 rules out any rebuilding of -200 or -220E engines – for example, the intermediate casing (the transition between the fan and the core) was redesigned.

To meet the needs of air forces which operate significant numbers of -200 and -220E powered aircraft, or which are denied security clearance to buy the -229, P&W has devised the F100-

PW-200+. This combines the core of the -220 with the fan, nozzle, and digital engine control system of the -229, and will develop around 27,000lb (12,250kg) of thrust. The -220E+ has already been proposed to the USAF as a potential upgrade to older F-15 and F-16 fighters.

On the export market, the higher

Below: The F-110-GE-110As were first delivered to the USAF in January 1985. The following year, they were installed in F-16-Cs and Ds.

thrust of the F110 made it the engine of choice through the mid to late 1980s. Arrival of the F100-PW-229 finally gave P&W the chance of re-entering the export market. In 1991, South Korea chose the F100-PW-229 for its licence-built F-16s, maintaining engine commonality with F-16Cs and Ds bought earlier from the USA.

When the US Government refused to fit the IPE engine to the Peace Marble II F-16s, Israel's Bet Shemesh Engine company developed its own improved F110.

This offers 50 per cent more thrust at low level, and is designated F110-GE-110A.

GE and P&W both have plans for further thrust increases. By increasing the internal temperatures of the engine, P&W has run a modified F100 engine at 31,000lb (14,000kg) rating, and -229 engines delivered in 1992 could well deliver more than 30,000lb (13,600kg).

Further thrust increases to around 34,000lb (15,400kg) are being studied, but would require a redesigned fan. In practice, this refanned F100 remains a

Above: Final adjustments are made to an F100 turbofan at the Pratt & Whitney works.

fallback design which is unlikely to be developed unless the USAF abandons the Lockheed F-22 Advanced Tactical Fighter and that aircraft's engine.

GE has its own refanning scheme, and hopes to obtain 35,000lb (15,875kg) in 1992 by modifying the F110 with a new fan based on that of the F118 engine used on the B-2 bomber.

Avionics

Advanced aerodynamics and a high thrust-to-weight ratio are not enough to make an advanced fighter. Without its complex payload of avionics 'black boxes', Fighting Falcon would not be able to search for and locate its targets under typically poor European weather conditions, or confuse hostile ground-based or airborne radars. And without the assistance of the complex fly-by-wire flight-control system, the F-16 pilot would probably be unable to cope with the inherent instability of his aircraft. With these systems installed, however, a basic lightweight fighter becomes a formidable multirole combat aircraft.

Like most US military aircraft, the F-16 carries a comprehensive suite of avionics. The basic installation in the F-16A/B is already greater than many proponents of the original Lightweight Fighter scheme may have envisaged, but this reflects the combat environment of the 1980s rather than any desire by GD or the USAF to 'gold plate' the aircraft. Under the MSIP and F-16C/D programmes even more systems will be added to improve all-weather capability. Some critics attack the Fighting Falcon as being over-complex, but the original concept of a simple day fighter is no longer suited to Western European operations.

Integration of the F-16 avionics makes extensive use of the MIL-STD-1553 multiplexed databus – a significant step forward in avionics design. The significance of computer languages and interfaces may seem obscure, but the complexity of modern warplanes makes standardization of these as important as the standardization of more tangible objects such as fixings, fastenings, connectors and weapon attachment points.

Traditional methods of avionics integration involved the use of bulky and expensive bundles of electric wiring for the distribution of signals and data. Multiplexing is a technique under which various equipments share a common electrical connection on a time-sampled basis – the electronic equivalent of time-sharing an apartment. If the number of times per second during which a signal has access to the electrical connection – databus – is sufficiently high compared with the rate at which that signal may change, the end result will be as acceptable as a fixed piece of wire. Lightweight digital switching electronics may therefore be substituted for heavy and bulky cabling.

Avionics standardization

By specifying an agreed 'code of conduct' for using the databus, MIL-STD-1553 greatly reduces the electronic interfacing problems experienced in earlier digital avionics systems, in which each manufacturer selected his own independent software (computer programs and instructions) as he saw fit.

GD was an enthusiastic supporter of avionics standardization, and all avionics for the F-16 were developed using a common interface and computer language. For the avionics improvements planned as part of the MSIP programme, the company standardized on the latest version of MIL-STD-1553, the Jovial computer language and a new standard interface for stores and stores-management systems.

The APG-66 radar

Primary target-detection sensor of the F-16 is the Westinghouse APG-66 radar. As originally conceived, the F-16 would have carried only a simple search set, probably similar in performance to that in the Northrop F-5E. Some individuals in the Department of Defense even suggested the use of a basic range-only unit with a fixed antenna.

Experience during the Vietnam War had shown how enemy aircraft could avoid detection by flying close to the ground, where the clutter experienced on normal pulse radars could hide them from observation. The need to have 'look-down' radar capability forced the adoption of a pulse-Doppler radar, but the traditional high complexity and cost of such equipment made the design of the much smaller APG-66 a difficult task.

In order to carry out a radar-controlled interception, an aircraft requires data on the bearing of the target and its range. Bearing can be measured by means of a highly-directional antenna giving good angular discrimination, but range data can most easily be obtained by pulsing the radar transmitter on and off again at a rate known as the pulse-repetition frequency (PRF). In the simpler types of radar equipment, sufficient time is allowed for one pulse to travel out to the target, be reflected, and return to the radar before the next pulse is transmitted. Engineers describe such radars as low-PRF sets.

Until the 1960s, airborne radars were almost blind when attempting to look downwards to detect low-flying aircraft. The latter were able to hide in the clutter produced by the strong radar echo from the terrain background against which they were being viewed.

Above: Westinghouse engineers install line-replaceable units in a development APG-66 radar to be test-flown in an F-4 Phantom.

Below: Marconi Avionics' holographic HUD begins flight trials in the front cockpit of an F-16B. The large combiner glass gives the unit the wide field-of-view needed for use with LANTIRN.

By the 1960s a new source of microwave power known as a travelling-wave tube (TWT), along with the use of digital signal processors, allowed the creation of pulse-Doppler radars with a good look-down performance.

The use of stable and coherent (phrase-related) pulses from a TWT allows the radar to measure the Doppler shift in the radar returns from the target – the tiny change in frequency caused by target motion relative to the signal source. Using this technique, the relative velocity of the target against the terrain background allowed the wanted target signal to be extracted from the massive background returns. This technique is known as pulse-Doppler radar.

TWT transmitters cannot match the high levels of power available from the magnetron transmitters used in low-PRF radars, so the designers were forced to use high PRFs in order to illuminate the target with sufficient power. Since each pulse would be transmitted before the previous pulse had completed the round trip out to a distant target and back, each pulse had to be electronically 'labelled' by a low-frequency modulation at the time of transmission.

Medium PRFs

The range data obtained by processing the labelled pulses is of low accuracy, and high PRFs are also poor at detecting targets whose closure rate is low. In the 1970s, therefore, designers of airborne radar turned to medium PRFs. These allow traditional methods of ranging to be used at most combat ranges, while still allowing pulse-Doppler techniques to be used for look-down operation.

Since the PRFs best suited to range measurement are different to those effective against low closing-rate targets, a practical design of medium-PRF set has to switch rapidly from one PRF value to another. This made the design of hardware able to carry out pulse-Doppler signal processing virtually impossible. The solution lay in the use of software-controlled digital signal processing. By making the characteristics of the filter dependent on a computer program (software) rather than physical components (hardware), the designers could contrive near-instantaneous re-configuration of the filter to match each PRF waveform used by the radar. The first radars to use medium PRFs and digital signal processors were the Hughes APG-65 in the F-15 Eagle and the L.M. Ericsson PS-46/A in the Viggen JA37 intercepter.

Below: The final FSD aircraft was temporarily fitted with a mock-up of an enlarged nose able to house the APG-65 radar used in the F/A-18.

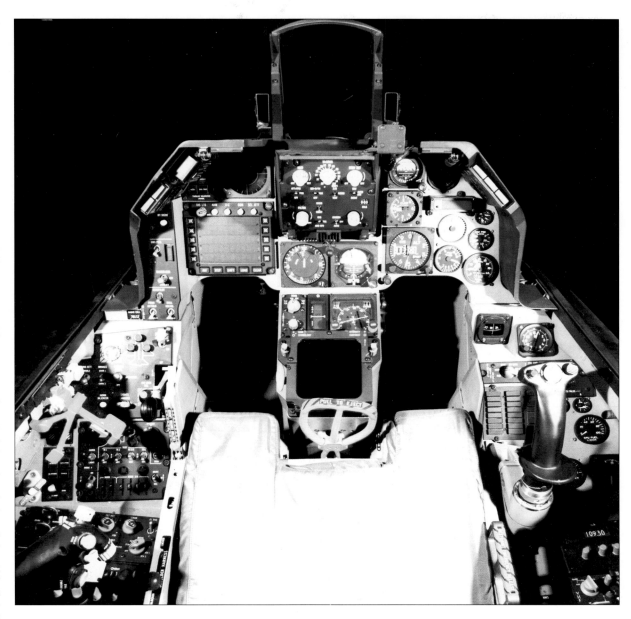

Development contracts for the F-16 radar were awarded to Hughes and Westinghouse, and both companies test-flew prototypes in a competitive evaluation before Westinghouse was awarded the contract for what became the APG-66. The specification was very demanding, calling for a medium-PRF pulse-Doppler set capable of being installed in the modestly-sized nose section of the Fighting Falcon.

The set was initially optimized for the air-to-air role, but air-to-surface modes were also requested soon after the fly-off. To minimize possible delays and cost increases, some compromises in air-to-ground performance were accepted. At high altitudes, for example, radar ground-mapping performance is lower than would have been possible with an antenna optimized for this role.

The APG-66 used in the F-16A/B is a medium-PRF radar (typically 10 to 15kHz). It operates in I/J band and incorporates a 'flat-plate' planar array antenna. Sixteen operating frequencies are available within the band, and the pilot may select between any four. Total weight is 296lb (134kg), and the set occupies a volume of 3.6cu ft (0.1cu m). A mean time between failures of 97 hours has been demonstrated.

Radar operating modes may be selected by the pilot using the throttle, sidestick controller or radar control panel. Like most modern sets, the APG-66 is designed so that all the controls needed during air combat are located

Above: Primary sources of nav/attack data for the F-16A pilot are the HUD (top) and square CRT display (between the pilot's knees).

on the control stick and throttle. When the set is tracking a target, the range scale is switched automatically to reduce pilot workload.

Primary air-combat mode is Downlook, which provides clutter-free indication of low-flying targets. Fighter-sized aircraft may be detected head- or tail-on at ranges of more than 30nm (34.5 miles/55.6km). If the target is flying at a higher altitude than the Fighting Falcon, the pilot may select Uplook mode, gaining a useful 33 per cent increase in detection range.

Below: Performance of the APG-66 radar against typical aircraft targets: the figures for the Soviet aircraft are estimates based on results with US types. Ranges obtained in look-up mode are better than those in look-down mode – in the latter case the set must carry out sophisticated signal processing to distinguish between the target and unwanted radar reflections from the ground.

Opposite: All controls needed during combat are mounted on the sidestick controller (top) and throttle (below). The Dogfight/MSL override switch on the latter can be set to the 'Dogfight' position to select radar Air Combat mode.

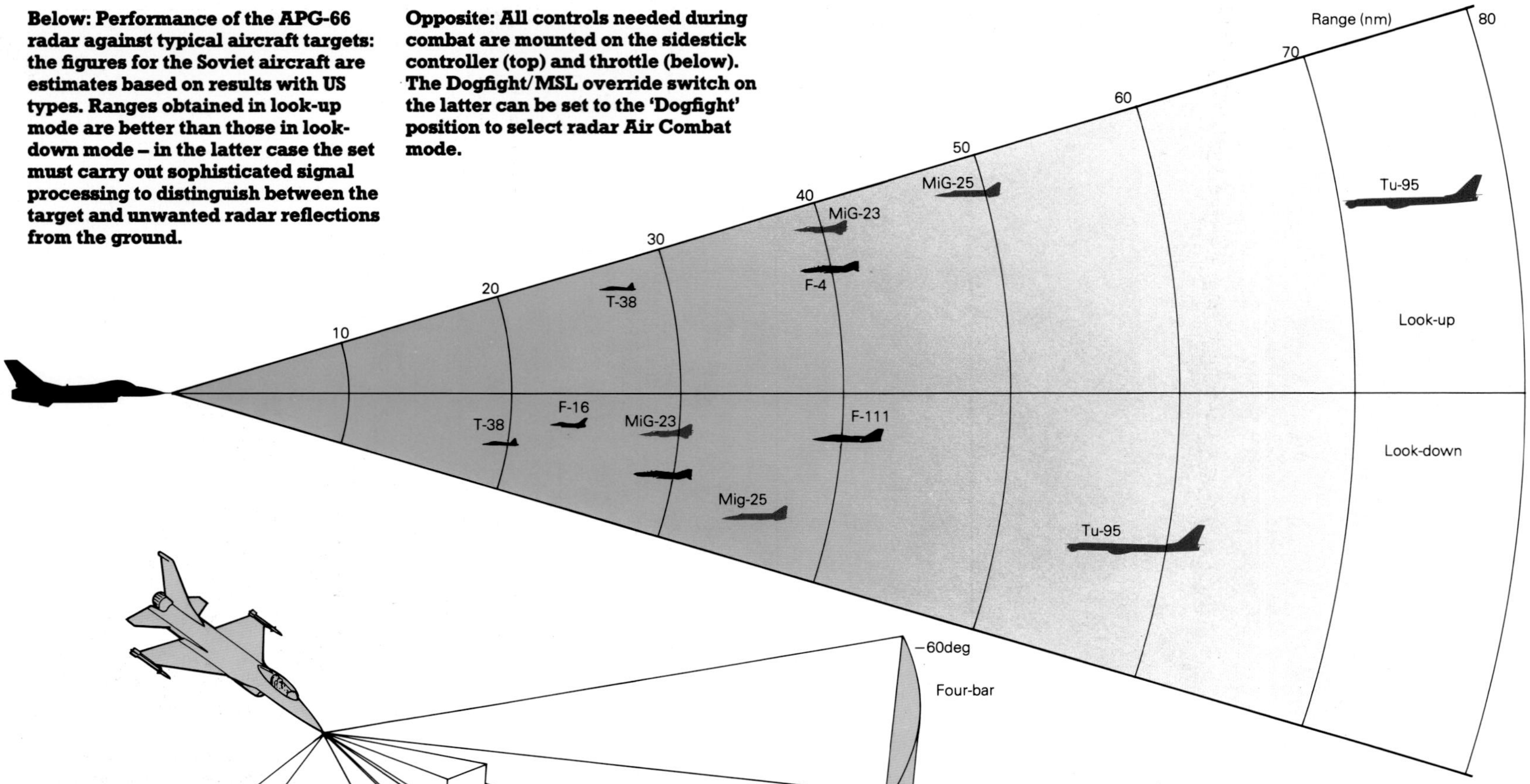

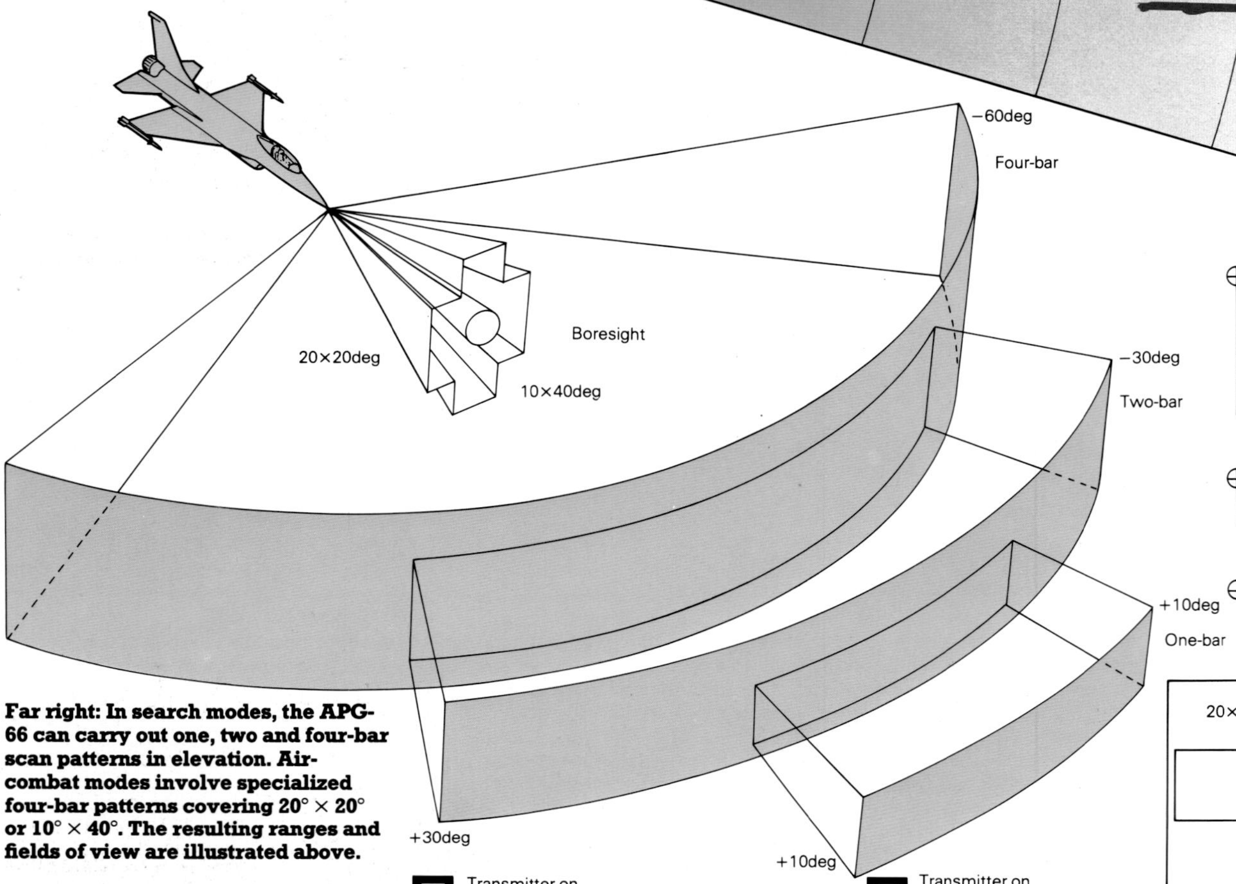

Range (nm)

80
70
60
50
40
30
20
10

Tu-95
MiG-25
MiG-23
F-4
T-38

Look-up

T-38
F-16
MiG-23
F-111

Look-down

Mig-25
Tu-95

—60deg
Four-bar

Boresight

−30deg
Two-bar

20×20deg
10×40deg

+10deg
One-bar

+30deg
+10deg

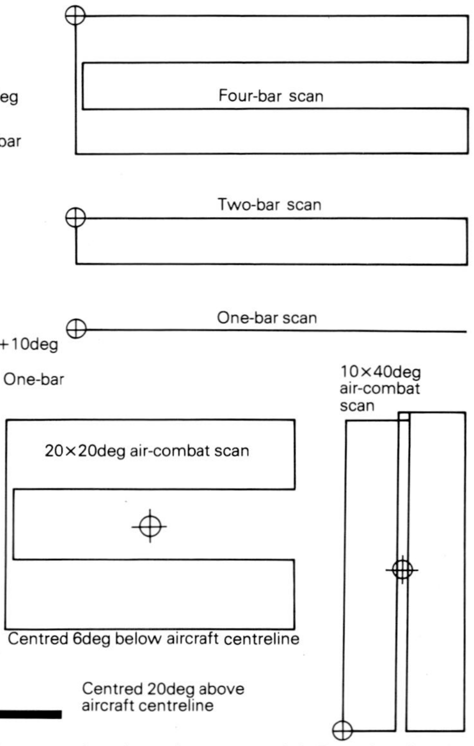

Transmitter on
Transmitter off

Transmitter on
Transmitter off

Four-bar scan

Two-bar scan

One-bar scan

10×40deg air-combat scan

20×20deg air-combat scan

Centred 6deg below aircraft centreline

Centred 20deg above aircraft centreline

Far right: In search modes, the APG-66 can carry out one, two and four-bar scan patterns in elevation. Air-combat modes involve specialized four-bar patterns covering 20° × 20° or 10° × 40°. The resulting ranges and fields of view are illustrated above.

Right: A pulse radar transmits for short periods of time only, spending the intervals listening for echoes from the target.

Four modes are available for air-to-air combat. In the Dogfight mode, selected by means of a throttle-mounted switch, the radar automatically scans a 20deg × 20deg field. If the pilot can see the target in his HUD, and the range is less than 10nm, the radar will automatically lock on. If high-g manoeuvres are to be carried out, the area to be searched can be altered to a 40deg × 10deg pattern.

If faced with several closely-spaced targets, the pilot can press the Designate button on his sidestick controller. The radar will then operate in a slim narrow-beam mode, and by manoeuvring his aircraft the pilot can place the beam on to the required target. When he releases the Designate switch, the radar will acquire and track the chosen victim.

Slewable air-combat mode can give the Fighting Falcon pilot the edge during combat manoeuvres. A cursor-control button on the throttle grip allows the scan pattern to be moved to anticipate target manoeuvres. This is particu-

larly useful when both aircraft are manoeuvring in the vertical plane.

Seven modes are provided for air-to-surface use. Air-to-ground ranging is automatically selected during continuously-computed impact point (CCIP) and dive-toss attacks, measuring the slant range to a designated point on the ground.

CCRP attacks

Continuously-computed release point (CCRP) attacks use the set's ground mapping modes. Real-beam ground mapping gives a plan position indicator (PPI) display at 10, 20, 40 or 80nm range, and scan widths of plus or minus 10deg, 30deg or 60deg. This image may be used for navigational updates, the location and detection of ground targets and for direct or offset weapon delivery.

Dedicated sea-surface search modes may be used in the maritime role. Sea 1 is a frequency-agile mode for use against stationary or moving vessels in up to sea state 4, while Sea 2 uses a narrow Doppler notch to detect moving

targets in higher sea states, and may also be used to indicate moving targets on land.

Beacon mode also uses a PPI display format. It may be used in conjunction with ground-located radar beacons to take navigation fixes or to carry out offset weapons delivery. In the air-to-air role, this mode is used to locate flight refuelling tankers by interrogating their beacons.

Several auxiliary methods of presenting imagery may be used in these PPI modes. If Freeze mode is selected, the radar carries out a final scan, the image of which is 'held' on the display, following which the radar transmitter is turned off so that the aircraft cannot be detected by passive means. A moving symbol on the display continues to indicate aircraft motion. Expanded-beam real map mode provides an optional ×4 magnification on all PPI modes. The pilot selects the 'patch' to be expanded from anywhere within the radar's scan and range limits.

Highest definition of ground features

is given by a special Doppler beam sharpened mode. Usable when the set is ground mapping at ranges of 10 or 20nm, this provides a further ×8 magnification over that in expanded-beam real map mode. Since this mode relies on the processing of Doppler shift, it is only available at angles between 15deg and 60deg off the aircraft's velocity vector. Should the aircraft's subsequent flight path bring the area being viewed to within 15deg of the aircraft centreline, the radar automatically switches to the normal ground-mapping mode. Doppler beam sharpening is likely to be much used when projected specialized off-boresight guided weapons finally enter service.

Development of an effective pulse-Doppler radar of such small size was a formidable technical undertaking, so it was hardly surprising that several problems were experienced during early tests, particularly in look-down mode. Pulse-Doppler radars measure the Doppler shift created by target velocity in order to discriminate between genuine

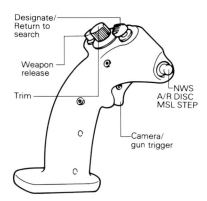

Designate/
Return to
search

Weapon
release

Trim

NWS
A/R DISC
MSL STEP

Camera/
gun trigger

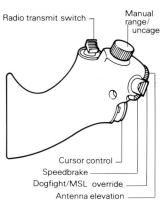

Radio transmit switch

Manual
range/
uncage

Cursor control
Speedbrake
Dogfight/MSL override
Antenna elevation

targets and ground clutter. This involves defining a threshold velocity – a speed at which targets must be moving in order to be accepted as valid. Vehicles on West German autobahns often move at speeds of 100mph (160km/h) or more, and were sometimes registered as low-level targets.

During tests over water in Norway, false targets registered on the radar were found to be due to stray radiation from the radar antenna. In designing an antenna, the engineer would like to see all of the signal being directed into the main beam, but in practice some always escapes in the form of sidelobes – unwanted weak beams at an angle to the main beam. A good design will reduce these sidelobes as much as possible, but it is virtually impossible to eliminate them. Radar energy escaping from these sidelobes was being reflected off the water in fjords, creating false targets.

Synthetic imagery

Earlier radars presented a direct radar picture to the operator, who could to some degree use his own skill and experience in deciding which targets were real. Sets such as the APG-66 reduce all radar data to digital form, and present the pilot with a synthetically generated image made up of pre-defined symbols. The screen is free from clutter and is much easier to read than that of earlier types of radar which showed 'raw' data, but the discrimination between real and false targets must be achieved automatically by signal-processing equipment. In the case of the early APG-66 sets, this feature required modification.

During other early trials, the radar

showed poor detection range and low performance in the Doppler beam-sharpened air-to-ground modes. Clearing up these and other 'bugs' took much time and effort, but the situation was under control by the summer of 1979. Modifications were made to the low-power RF circuitry, digital signal processor and system software, and the revised equipment was under flight test and evaluation by the end of 1979.

Improvements to the APG-66 form part of the MSIP update programme. In 1980 Westinghouse was awarded a $25 million contract to begin development

of a programmable signal processor (PSP) and dual-mode transmitter for the APG-66. The latter would use low PRFs for air-to-ground work, and medium to high PRFs in air-to-air combat. These modifications were intended to match the performance of the AMRAAM missile, and to improve air-to-ground capability and ECCM performance. The set would also receive track-while-scan and raid-assessment modes. Both new sub-units were designed to occupy the same space as the equipment they replaced.

The design of TWTs able to operate

Above: If the one-piece canopy were to fail, the combiner glass of the HUD would act as a windshield.

efficiently over a wide range of PRFs is difficult. Given low or even medium PRFs, the transmitting tube of a radar spends more time silent than transmitting. In engineering jargon, the 'duty cycle' of time 'off' to time 'on' is low. The tube thus has plenty of time to cool between individual pulses, so the designer can work the device hard while it is actually radiating, obtaining high levels of peak power.

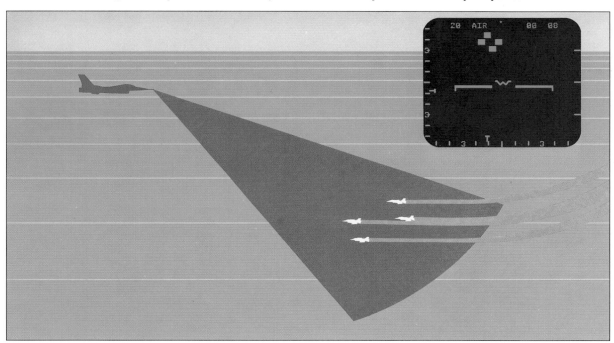

Above right: Primary air-to-air radar mode is Downlook, a medium-PRF search and track mode able to detect low-flying intruders. According to Westinghouse, the set has a low false-alarm rate of less than two per minute. The radar displays use computer-generated alphanumeric and other symbology, to present the pilot with clean imagery, while the effects of clutter and system noise are filtered out by signal processing. Earlier-generation radars presented 'raw' analogue radar imagery to the user, requiring skilled interpretation.

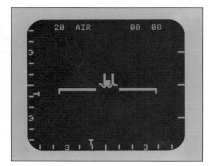

Range scale
Mode
Target altitude, 4,000ft MSL

Horizon line

Target symbol (track)

Target data block: Target's ground track
Target's calibrated airspeed
Aspect angle for intercept

Closure rate

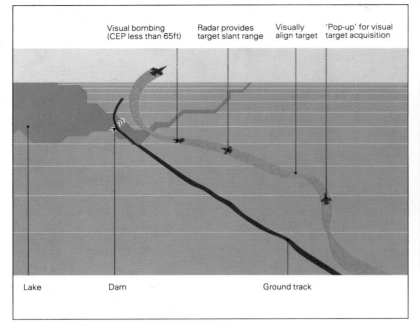

| Visual bombing (CEP less than 65ft) | Radar provides target slant range | Visually align target | 'Pop-up' for visual target acquisition |

Lake   Dam   Ground track

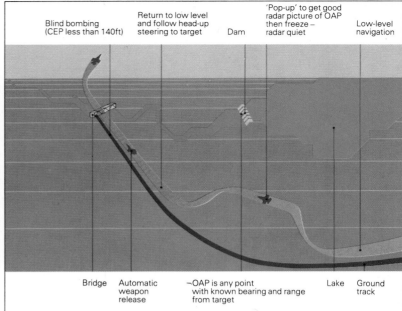

| Blind bombing (CEP less than 140ft) | Return to low level and follow head-up steering to target | Dam | 'Pop-up' to get good radar picture of OAP then freeze – radar quiet | Low-level navigation |

Bridge   Automatic weapon release   ¬OAP is any point with known bearing and range from target   Lake   Ground track

Above: During CCIP (continuously-computed impact point) attacks, the APG-66 radar is used to measure slant range to the target during the final run.

At high PRFs, the tube spends much more of its time transmitting, and has less time to cool down between pulses, involving a duty cycle of 50 per cent or more. As a result, the amount of power which can be extracted in each individual pulse is reduced.

By the time that Westinghouse faced the problem of updating the APG-66, its great rival in the airborne radar business had developed a new type of TWT which made dual-mode operation much more efficient. Working in conjunction with Litton, Hughes had created a TWT able to cope with the high peak-power demands of low- and medium-PRF operation, while still operating efficiently at the high duty cycles required by high PRFs. Long-range detection performance at medium PRFs could now match that at high PRFs.

All-round improvements

All F-16C and D aircraft carry the improved APG-68 radar. This uses new dual-mode tube technology to provide low, medium and high PRFs, and to deliver more transmitted power in air-to-air combat. The low-power RF section of the radar was redesigned to use plug-in assemblies.

The APG-66 radar on NATO F-16s has

Above right: CCRP (continuously-computed release point) attacks use the the ground mapping radar modes. A radar map may be created and 'frozen' during a pop-up manoeuvre.

separate hardwired signal and data processors, but on the -68 this is replaced by a single software-controlled programmable signal processor (PSP). Based on VHSIC (Very High Speed Integrated Circuit) technology, this handles both signal and data processing.

The APG-68 has longer-ranged tactical modes and the ability to fire radar-guided missiles at BVR (beyond visual range) targets, while the improved data processing allows the set to track multiple targets, detect and track moving and anchored surface ships, and provide 8:1 and 64:1 high-resolution mapping modes. It can also handle the AIM-120A AMRAAM missile.

In air-to-air combat, three of the radar's most useful features are track-while-scan, raid cluster resolution, and ACM (air-combat manoeuvring) mode. Track-while-scan allows the radar to maintain tracks of several high-priority targets, and marking that with the highest priority, while continuing to search for others. Raid cluster resolution allows the pilot to distinguish between the individual aircraft in a tight formation at long range, while ACM mode allows the radar to follow hard-manoeuvring targets at short range.

For Block 50 aircraft, a further

upgrade is planned. This will be able to handle several types of advanced radar modes. Another development on the avionics drawing board is a low-power RF assembly with a second channel for monopulse operation to provide a guard channel. This modification will also involve changes to the receiver and stable local oscillator.

LORO

In its current form, the radar uses Lobe On Receive Only (LORO), with the receive beam switching in a random sequence between four positions to provide a cheap solution to the problem of angular tracking.

The traditional method of providing monopulse capability – the ability to measure angle with a single pulse – is to provide four channels measuring sum and difference in both elevation and azimuth. This adds size and weight, so for the APG-68, Westinghouse will use the two channels to allow the radar to switch between an elevation and azimuth difference pattern.

A mid-life update programme is also being applied to the APG-66 radar of the F-16A and B. The separate hardwired signal and data processors will be replaced by a new signal data processor which combines the functions of both units. The replacement is smaller, lighter and requires less power and cooling, yet has seven times the processing speed and seven times the non-volatile memory.

The LANTIRN programme

In the late 1980s, the APG-66 will be backed up by the Martin Marietta LANTIRN (low-Altitude Navigation and Targeting Infra-Red for Night) system. This equipment will allow the pilot of a single-seat aircraft to fly sorties by day or night and in adverse weather. It can provide terrain-following radar and FLIR (forward-looking infra-red) imagery for navigation; automatically acquire, identify and categorize tank targets, passing target information to the aircraft's fire-control system so that Maverick missiles may be launched against several targets in a single pass; and can acquire and track fixed ground targets using FLIR or visual techniques, then designate them for attack using a built-in laser.

The basic installation comprises two avionics pods containing the sensors for navigation and target acquisition/tracking respectively. Martin Marietta is prime contractor for both. On the F-16, the pods will be carried on hardpoints under the inlet. They can operate autonomously, so an aircraft could fly into action with only one should this meet the requirements of the mission. Although the programme was formally launched in 1980, it was suspended just over a year later, and reshaped to reduced the technical risks involved.

The navigation pod is 12in (30.5cm) in diameter, 78in (198cm) long and weighs about 430lb (195kg). Main subsystems are a Ku-band terrain-following radar, wide field-of-view FLIR, pod computer and the associated power supply. Sophisticated signal processing is used to give the radar a wide azimuth coverage, allowing high-rate turns at low level in order to avoid or confuse the defences. This should give greater survivability than earlier-generation equipments which simply issued pitch commands. The latter may have allowed him to avoid the terrain ahead, but exposed the aircraft to ground fire.

FLIR field of view is 28deg in azimuth and 21deg in elevation. The resulting wide-angle imagery may be superimposed on the outside scene by means of the HUD. In darkness or bad weather the HUD provides an image of TV-like quality and sufficient width to allow the pilot to look in the direction of his turn in order to 'preview' the terrain.

Targeting pod

The larger targeting pod has a movable nose section containing a FLIR sensor, laser transmitter/receiver and a stabilization system able to compensate for aircraft movements and vibration. A

LANTIRN navigation pod (right) and targeting pod (below)

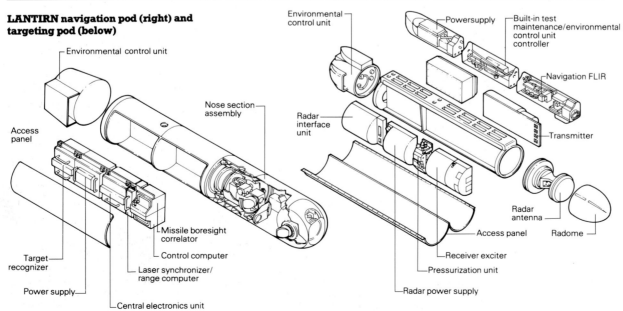

fixed centre section houses the tracker electronics and signal-processing systems and the boresight correlator used to pass target data to the aircraft's air-to-ground weapons. Environmental control of these systems and the nose-section sensors is handled by equipment in the aft section of the pod.

Flight testing using dummy fairings began in September 1982. The simulated pods have the same weight and mass distribution as the actual equipment and were instrumented to allow measurements of flutter, vibration and loads to be carried out. Test flying with functional equipment was scheduled to begin in the summer of 1983 using two F-16B and two A-10A trials aircraft. By the winter of 1984, LANTIRN equipment is scheduled to have completed tests under adverse operating conditions during combined development test and evaluation/initial operational test and evaluation trials in Europe.

In a typical LANTIRN attack, the aircraft will perform a 'pop-up' manoeuvre at the initial point. Scanning to either side of the flight path, the sensors pass IR imagery to the target-recognition systems. Once targets have been assessed, they will be shown to the pilot on his head-down display, while the HUD marks the first to be engaged. Using a second cockpit CRT display to show IR imagery from the Maverick missiles, the pilot will assign the first round to its target. As one round is launched, the system will automatically set up for the next, allowing up to six targets to be engaged during a single pass. LANTIRN can also handle laser-guided munitions. In this case, the system would illuminate the pre-selected target as the aircraft pulled up and released its weapon.

If the aircraft is fitted with the LANTIRN targeting pod, this gives a better IR image than the AGM-65D seeker. This increases the stand-off range during night attacks, and reduces the time needed to lock on the missile seeker.

The LANTIRN HUD is made by GEC Marconi Avionics, and combines traditional HUD symbology with raster-scanned (TV-style) display of imagery from the EO system. Close attention has been paid to the needs of air combat. The HUD can act as a simple lead-computing optical sight (LCOS), an expanded-envelope gun sight (EEGS), plus providing snap-shoot and AIM-9 slaving. Most of the controls the pilot might need in combat are mounted on a small panel on front of the HUD just below the combiner glass. Using these, he can input data to the fire-control system, control the FLIR, and change radio channels or IFF modes.

Combat debut

First combat use of the system came during the 1991 Gulf War, but priority was given to equipping the F-15E force. The F-15Es assigned to Desert Storm carried the AAQ-13 LANTIRN navigation pod plus a smaller number of AAQ-14 LANTIRN targeting pods. Of the 249 F-16s sent to the Gulf, 72 were equipped with the AAQ-13 LANTIRN.

Four export F-16C/D operators have already purchased LANTIRN systems, and one has purchased the Pathfinder/Sharpshooter combination. Interest is being shown by two other F-16C/D users and one F-16A/B user.

The AAQ-20 Pathfinder is an export variant of LANTIRN – essentially an AAQ-13 navigation pod without the terrain-following radar but with a FLIR that offers up to x3 magnification, a slewable line of sight, plus an optional zoom. The companion AAQ-14(V) Sharpshooter targeting pod lacks the missile boresight correlator of the standard AAQ-14.

One improvement planned for Pathfinder is an algorithmic-based target cuer. Automatic target recognition was a feature originally planned for LANTIRN, but has always been seen as a risky venture given the state of early 1980s electronic technology. Hughes and Martin Marietta worked on rival designs of Automatic Target Recogniser, but planned to install this capability in LANTIRN were shelved.

Already demonstrated in laboratory and tower trials, the new Pathfinder cuer was in flight test by 1991. When it enters service, the pilot will be able to select variables such as target size and range, target priority, and relative intensity, and the system will display up to ten targets.

Cockpit displays

Data from the radar and Nav/attack systems of the Fighting Falcon are presented to the pilot on head-up and head-down displays. In the F-16A and B the head-down CRT display is manufactured by Kaiser, but for the HUD the USAF turned to the British company Marconi Avionics. A specialist in HUD technology, this Rochester-based company created the first HUD to enter service on a production aircraft – the Hawker Siddeley Buccaneer – back in 1960, and subsequently became an established supplier of HUDs to the USAF, building units for the A-7 Corsair II.

The original Buccaneer unit was primitive by modern standards, using analogue electronics and simple symbology. The A-7 HUD used digital electronics for computing and the positioning of the symbology, establishing the style of HUD now produced by many companies around the world. More than 2,000 units have been delivered for the Corsair II, and one of the company's HUDs was removed from the wreckage of an A-7 shot down in Vietnam, returned to the UK and found to be still in working order.

In addition to supplying the USAF, Marconi Avionics also provides equipment for other advanced military aircraft such as the Panavia Tornado, and

had even developed the HUD for the Mirage F1.E contender for the NATO fighter order. For the Fighting Falcon programme, the UK company was involved from the beginning, having been awarded a contract to develop HUDs for the original two YF-16 prototypes. All subsequent patterns of HUD flown on or planned for the F-16 were designed by the same team.

In developing the F-16 HUD, the company placed great emphasis on the air-to-air gunnery role, aiming to create a system capable of giving a good first-burst hit probability. Radar ranging would normally be used, but a rotary switch on the HUD front panel provides for the more traditional stadiametric ranging, using the known wing span of the target as a reference from which to compute range.

Since the entire canopy of the F-16 is a one-piece polycarbonate component, its loss in an accident or in preparation for ejection would expose the pilot to

Above: A wide-angle HUD and two multipurpose CRT head-down displays are the main features of the F-16C/D cockpit. The British-developed HUD can superimpose IR imagery on the external scene.

the full force of the slipstream. Design of the optical components of the HUD was contracted to the UK company Pilkington PPE, whose designers ensured that the combiner glass of the unit was strong enough to withstand the slipstream. With the canopy gone, the HUD can thus act as a temporary windshield.

Field of view of the F-16A/B HUD is 13·5deg in azimuth by 9deg in elevation. For the AFTI project a wider field of view was required, so the Rochester design team pushed conventional optical technology to its limits to produce an impressive 20 × 15deg field. For use with the LANTIRN pod, the USAF asked for a HUD with an even larger field – 30 × 20deg. This forced the design team

Above: Marconi Avionics (now renamed GEC Avionics) developed the wide-angle HUD used to present LANTIRN imagery to the pilot of an F-16C or D. Its small front panel contains the controls the pilot will need in combat situations.

Above: Standard Marconi Avionics head-up display in an F-16A. The rectangular display seen below and to the left of the HUD control panel is not a radar display but forms part of the Fighting Falcon's sophisticated stores-management system.

to return to the first principles of optics and devise an entirely new type of display.

The constraints on the HUD designer include the need to interfere as little as possible with the pilot's field of view, to take up as little of the instrument panel as possible, and not to intrude beyond the confines set by the windscreen and the ejection line. The last boundary is set by the space needed by the pilot's legs and feet during ejection.

To maximize the field of view the designer could mount the combiner glass as close to the ejection line as possible. This leaves no room for the traditional pattern of CRT image-injection system, since the latter is mounted on the pilot's side of the combiner glass and would thus project over the ejection line. A complex optical path involving 'folding' the light rays was devised, but this had a low efficiency, resulting in a dim view of both the CRT-generated imagery and the outside world.

The final solution entailed the use of a combiner consisting of a reflective hologram or diffraction grating to create the effect of a mirror surface. Holograms reflect light of only a certain colour, allowing light of all other colours to pass freely. In the LANTIRN HUD design, the colour chosen for reflection is the green associated with the CRT used to generate symbology. The combiner can thus act simultaneously as an efficient mirror and as a transparency. To quote Robin Sleight, Technical Manager of the Marconi Airborne Displays division, "We have found one of the rare conditions in life where we are getting something for nothing: a surface which transmits 90 per cent of the light hitting it, yet apparently also reflects to a similar value!"

The first unit was handed over to the USAF in March 1982, and flight tests

Above: The wide-angle HUD devised for the AFT1/F-16 forms the basis of the F-16C HUD. This design offers the widest field of view possible using conventional optics.

aboard an F-16 started the same summer. Like the LANTIRN system itself, the holographic HUD faces an uncertain future. Early in 1983 Marconi Avionics announced that it had been awarded a contract to build a new pattern of HUD for the F-16C and D, but this is largely based on the AFTI unit rather than on the holographic design. It seems likely that the new unit will be modified for use with LANTIRN.

Under the MSIP programme, the F-16 will also receive new patterns of head-down cockpit displays. General Dynamics will install a moving-map display on an instrument panel between the pilot's knees, displacing conventional mechanical standby flight instruments. This system was chosen in preference to the synthetic raster-scan display favoured by GD, which would have allowed moving-map data to be displayed on any of three multi-function cockpit CRT displays being developed by Sperry.

ECM systems

In addition to its offensive avionics, the Fighting Falcon is equipped with defensive electronic countermeasures (ECM) systems intended to help it survive in the face of modern air defences. Secrecy is essential if ECM techniques and tactics are to remain effective, so very little detailed information has been published concerning the performance of the equipment mentioned below.

The most basic item of ECM equipment is the radar-warning receiver (RWR). This is designed to detect the signals from hostile radars, and to alert

the pilot that he is under observation. Most patterns of RWR give an approximate indication of the threat bearing, frequency and signal characteristics, while some identify the threat using a built-in catalogue of threat parameters.

When a threat radar is first detected by the RWR, the threat may not yet have detected the incoming aircraft. The RWR has the relatively simple task of detecting the powerful signal transmitted by the hostile radar, but the receiving system of the latter must attempt to detect the small amount of energy reflected by the target.

The threat radar will almost certainly be fitted with a relatively large and highly-directional antenna, while the RWR has only a low-gain omni-directional antenna array, but despite this inequality the RWR will usually detect the radar before the latter has detected the aircraft. Given this warning, the pilot may change course to avoid the radar, reduce cruise height in order to fly beneath the radar's horizon, or turn on some form of ECM. The warning provided by the RWR gives him a clear advantage.

The same techniques may be used if a tracking radar manages to lock on to the aircraft. The RWR display will probably give the first indication to the pilot that his tactics have been successful in 'breaking the lock' of the hostile system.

Basic RWR carried by the F-16 is the Itek ALR-69. Based on the earlier ALR-46, this was developed for the USAF and US Navy and consists of five general-purpose surveillance receivers plus a sixth frequency-selective receiver. The latter is probably used to detect signals associated with semi-active homing missile systems such as the Soviet SA-6 Gainful, and gives an indication of the direction of attack.

The US desire to limit exports of this sensitive equipment led to Pakistan rejecting its first batch of F-16s in 1982. These were to have been fitted with the Itek ALR-46. Widely exported to nations such as Egypt, Iran, Portugal, Saudi Arabia, South Korea, Switzerland, Taiwan, Thailand and West Germany, the ALR-46 covers the radar spectrum from 2.0 to 18GHz. Alarm indications are given on CRT cockpit displays and in the pilot's headset. Pakistan was eventually cleared to receive the ALR-69, but the older equipment may still be supplied to F-16 operators who do not face the most sophisticated threat systems.

At a later date, USAF aircraft could receive the latest RWR currently under development, the Itek ALR-74. This uses some of the technology developed for the US Navy's ALR-69, and is intended to counter Soviet threats anticipated for the late 1980s. Both programmes have attracted criticism from the US GAO, which wants to see a common RWR developed for both services.

Many F-16 operators have already opted to fit their aircraft with further ECM protection in the form of active jamming systems or chaff dispensers. The equipment selected is often specific to the individual air arm, although a degree of standardization is being attempted

Modern jamming systems operate in noise and deception modes. Noise jamming aims to swamp the hostile radar signal or communications link with unwanted radio-frequency noise, so that the genuine and wanted signal cannot be distinguished from the background. The technique is simple to implement, since very little needs to be known about the characteristics of the threats. If the exact operating frequency of the latter is known, the jammer may be pre-tuned to concentrate its output power on these frequencies. This is known as spot jamming.

If the threat frequency is not known exactly, or if the threat is frequency-agile, the simplest technique is to radiate the noise output of the jammer over a range of frequencies likely to contain the threat. This is known as barrage jamming, and is a simple technique, but the need to spread the power of the jammer reduces its effectiveness. Since the aircraft-mounted system can only generate a relatively modest level of jamming power, the signal-to-noise ratio received by the threat radar or system will be much lower than with spot jamming, easing the task of filtering out the wanted signal from the unwanted.

Rather than attempt such brute-force solutions, the modern jamming system uses a built-in search (or 'set-on') receiver to monitor the frequency of all detected threat signals. The output from this receiver may be used to control the frequency of the jammer transmitters, so that the spot jamming may be used against a threat of unknown or variable frequency.

Deceptive jamming

More complex patterns of monitoring receiver may be used to allow subtler forms of jamming – a family of techniques known as deceptive jamming. These involve receiving the threat signal, processing it in some way, then re-transmitting it in the hope of persuading the threat system to accept the doctored signal as genuine. By choosing the manner in which the signal is processed before transmission, the ECM designer can feed false range or bearing information to an enemy radar, or even cause multiple false targets to be detected.

Demonstrating such false target jamming to the author several years ago, Westinghouse technicians effectively blanked out the circular PPI (plan-position indicator) display of a surveillance radar by generating thousands of false targets simultaneously. So closely were these spaced on the display that the CRT face literally turned an even shade of white.

In a modern jamming system the search receiver monitors all radar signals received, comparing their parameters with a built-in threat library. Once those representing the greatest threat to the aircraft have been identified, the jammer assigns the power available from its various jamming transmitters accordingly. This technique is known as power-management.

The type of jamming to be used will be chosen to match the threat, and the receiver will often monitor the hostile transmission at regular intervals in order to assess the effect of its jamming. If the latter is not proving effective, a different jamming method may be automatically selected.

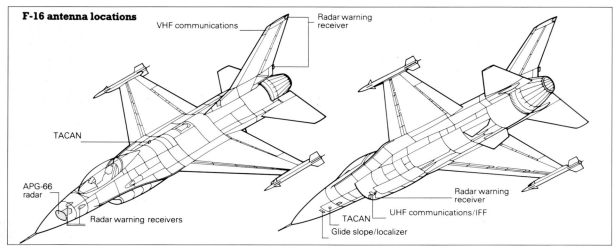

F-16 antenna locations

VHF communications

Radar warning receiver

TACAN

APG-66 radar

Radar warning receivers

TACAN

UHF communications/IFF

Radar warning receiver

Glide slope/localizer

In the early stages of the full-scale development programme, Tactical Air Command contemplated an internal ECM system. Studies of possible aircraft installations were carried out, and the likely balance between cost and aircraft survivability assessed. It was appreciated that an internal system would require the use of new technology and would take some time to develop and deploy.

All external stores had to be flutter tested, and some problem was initially experienced with the ALQ-119 ECM pod. When the aircraft was loaded with one specific configuration of stores, a speed limit had to be imposed. Tests with the ALQ-131 showed that carriage of the more modern pod required no such restraint.

Both the USAF and the Royal Netherlands Air Force adopted the ALQ-131 pod for the protection of their F-16 force. Selection of an ECM system for the F-16 became a major political issue in the Netherlands, with the Christian Democrat/Liberal coalition Government supporting the ALQ-131 and the Labour party being opposed to its adoption. The controversy was marked by Parliamentary hearings and debates. The US offer in August 1980 of a batch of 75 ALQ-131 ECM pods at a total cost of $63.5 million was the final factor which persuaded the RNethAF to adopt the standard USAF pod. This was seen as being cheaper than an internal ECM fit, and offered the advantages of standardization within NATO. Denmark and Norway were due to select an ECM fit in 1981, but lack of defense funds made it likely that no ECM would be fitted.

Development of the ALQ-131 started in the early 1970s to meet a USAF requirement. Following successful development and flight tests, the unit was ordered into production in 1976. ALQ-131 is a 573lb (260kg) modular pod-mounted system able to cope with a wide range of threats, particularly the radars and guidance systems of air-defence systems.

By selecting internal modules, the user may configure the pod to handle threats spread over one to five frequency bands. Modules are available to cope with all frequencies used by current anti-aircraft missile systems, and both noise and deception-jamming modes are available. The pod is power-managed, and the software can easily be modified to cope with the tactical situation which the user faces, or to take into account changes in threat tactics or parameters. Such modifications may be easily carried out, and may even be implemented on the flight line.

The struggle between the ECM designer and the latest tactics and systems is a continuous one. If the prospective enemy introduces new radar bands or techniques, hardware modifications may be needed. The USAF initiated the classified Have Exit update programme in 1980, four years after the equipment entered service. In this case, the system was probably being updated to cope with new Soviet threat systems featuring monopulse radars.

The USAF carries the ALQ-131 pod on the fuselage centreline hardpoint, thus losing the ability to carry an additional 300US gal (360Imp gal/1637l) of external fuel. It also left internal space available for follow-on systems such as AMRAAM-related equipment and the JTIDS (Joint Tactical Information Distribution System) data terminal.

The Rapport III system

After a study of the merits of pod-mounted and internal ECM systems, the Belgian Air Force decided in 1979 to adopt the Loral Rapport III (Rapid Alert

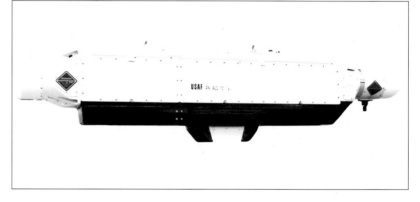

Above: If pod-mounted electronic countermeasures are carried on the F-16, the ventral hardpoint is normally used. This 388th TFW aircraft is equipped with a Westinghouse ALQ-119, almost certainly the (V)-12 version.

Right: Main recognition features of the Westinghouse ALQ-131 ECM pod are the full-length ventral gondola and two ventrally-mounted antennae. The red and black markings near the fore and aft-mounted radomes warn personnel to keep at least 15ft (4.6m) away when the pod is transmitting.

Programmed Power Management of Radar Target) internal ECM suite. The original version of Rapport was developed for the FAéB following a study of the Mirage 5B carried out in the light of Israeli experience during the 1973 Middle East War.

Requests for proposals for an internal ECM installation were circulated to US and European electronics companies early in 1974. Three companies were contracted to carry out feasibility studies, a team consisting of Loral and MBLE being chosen to develop the prototype Rapport II.

Belgium demonstrated Rapport II to its NATO F-16 partners, but failed to arouse much interest. It then funded GD to carry out a study of a Rapport installation for the F-16. The GD response was favourable, so contracts for two prototypes of the Rapport III system for the F-16 were awarded to Loral and GD in 1979. Part of the system is carried in an extended fairing at the base of the tail fin. Rapport III is designed to be compatible with the Rapport II equipment still carried by Belgian Mirage 5R and 5BA fighters.

Before adopting Rapport the Belgian Air Force studied rival equipments, but concluded that the former system was likely to be cheaper than alternative US equipments. Being internally mounted, Rapport also has the advantage of not taking up a hardpoint and does not add to aircraft drag. One penalty which Belgium was forced to pay was the loss of internal avionics growth space, and the fact that the packaging of future avionics adopted by the NATO F-16 users would be non-standard on Belgian aircraft.

Flight trials of Rapport III were carried out during the summer of 1981 at

Right: Aircraft cruising at medium altitude should be sitting ducks for hostile defences, but the ALQ-131 pod's noise and deception jammers can counter all known SAM systems.

Eglin AFB, Florida, using two Belgian Air Force F-16s. Units were flown against simulated threat systems and other equipment at the Eglin EW range.

The USAF did not carry out a full test of the equipment itself, but concluded from limited studies that the effectiveness of the ALQ-131 and Rapport III were broadly comparable. Minor technical problems delayed completion of the test programme, and while the equipment was shown to meet all requirements, the delays resulted in an overrun in the trials budget.

This increased cost posed strains of what was already a tightly-funded programme, so Belgium was faced with the option of either voting additional funds, or reducing the number of aircraft to be fitted from the planned 72. To save money, only 56 aircraft were scheduled to receive Rapport III.

The programme struggled on through the mid-1980s, but Belgium's chronic shortage of defence funds, plus possible problems in transferring the necessary technology from the US to Belgium eventually doomed that nation's order. Cancellation was announced in September 1988.

This decision left the Belgian Air Force without an EW suite for its F-16 fleet. In 1989, Belgium ordered the much simpler Electronique Serge Dassault Carapace passive EW, whose lower cost should allow installation on the entire F-16 fleet.

Two customers did buy Rapport III. Turkey adopted the system for its licence-built F-16C/D fleet, while an earlier order was placed in 1983 by an unidentified customer, thought to be Israel.

In 1979 the US Congress ordered the USAF and US Navy to evaluate Rapport III, but both declined to adopt the system. The USAF rejected Rapport III, pointing out that it was incompatible with the ALR-69 RWR, while the USN described the system as 'entirely unacceptable'. Both services were already collaborating on the inter-service Advanced Self-Protection Jammer (ASPJ) project.

Development of the ASPJ started as a competition between two industrial groups, with Westinghouse and ITT eventually defeating the Northrop/Sanders team. Space for ASPJ was always available within the F-16, but ECP350

Left: Lear-Siegler voice-control system from F-16/AFTI.
Below: Infra-red image obtained from the Oldelft Orpheus recce pod, to be used by RNethAF F-16s.

Above: The USAF has no current plans to deploy a dedicated reconnaissance version of the F-16, but the 6th full-scale development aircraft was flown with a dummy camera pod.

introduced the necessary internal holes and ducts for the system's waveguides and wiring.

So advanced is the design of the ALQ-165 ASPJ that the job was thought impossible by many people, according to Westinghouse. The Services were determined to obtain a system which would not suffer from early obsolescence as the threat systems it faced were updated. The designers decided to sever the pre-set relationship between threat and countermeasure which has been a feature of earlier ECM systems, and to rely on the ASPJ computer to select the appropriate countermeasure techniques in accordance with a combination of established threat data and real-time information obtained from the system's built-in receiver/signal processor.

The operational requirement called for ASPJ to cover several octaves of frequency, handling multiple threat signals against a dense background of other signals. The system can simultaneously jam many threats using its power-managed dual-mode transmitters. These have parallel TWT tubes which can be used to cope with pulse or CW signals in response to demands from the system software.

Just as the system was about to enter production, the USAF pulled out of the programme. The main reason given at the time was lack of money for such a complex and expensive system, but behind the scenes the USAF was

becoming increasingly convinced that the high cost and complexity of modern airborne jammers was coming at a time when ECCM techniques were becoming more sophisticated, and threatening to blunt the effectiveness of EW. systems. For the moment, USAF F-16s must rely on the ALQ-131 and the newer Raytheon ALQ-184 pod.

Communications equipment

Basic communications installation in the F-16A and B consists of Collins ARC-186 VHF AM/FM and Magnavox ARC-164 UHF transceivers, a Magnavox KY-58 secure voice system and an interference blanker by Novatronics. Between 1984 and 1986 the USAF F-16 force will be equipped with the new JTIDS jam-resistant command, control and communications system, plus the Seek Talk ECM-resistant voice-communications equipment should this survive budget cut-backs.

Part of the MSIP Phase III programme, these units will be introduced at the same time as the LANTIRN electro-optical system, AMRAAM missile and the ASPJ electronic countermeasures system. Also introduced around this time will be new navigation equipment which will utilise the GPS satellite system. This will supplement the current Singer-Kearfott-developed SKN-2000 inertial navigation system.

One unusual item of communications equipment being pioneered in the AFTI/F-16 is a Lear-Siegler voice-con-

trol system. Designated Voice-Controlled Interactive Device (VCID), this is used to control the AFTI avionic systems. In its initial form the VCID system has a vocabulary of 32 words, but this will eventually expand to a maximum of 256. Early tests used words such as 'menu', 'data', 'entry', 'plus', 'minus', and 'recall', plus numbers, phonetic letters, and the points of the compass.

In the early stages of AFTI flight tests only single-word commands were used. These control nav/attack and flight-control modes, and later tests will evaluate the use of connected phrases. There are no plans at present to use voice command to handle critical safety-related functions such as primary flight control or weapon release.

In theory, electronic systems should be able to deal with complete sentences, searching for and extracting the relevant nouns and verbs. This type of parsing operation – a development of artificial intelligence research – can already be done via the keyboard of all but the smallest computers, and has been incorporated into computerized 'adventure' games such as Zork.

One problem with voice-recognition systems is that not only are they voice dependent – that is, they tend to respond accurately only to the voice for which they were set up – but that the accuracy also depends on voice characteristics remaining, if not constant, at least predictable. To explore this area GD conducted tests to see how

voice quality changes owing to factors such as time of day, stress, fatigue, and G-loading. Other tests explored the effect on voice-operated systems of extraneous noise in the aircraft cockpit or in the pilot's oxygen mask, for example.

Noise level in the cockpit of a high-performance aircraft is very high; in the F-16 it can exceed 120dB during 9g manoeuvres. High g forces also make speech difficult or even impossible. During GD centrifuge tests, few pilots could talk at levels of more than 5g, although one individual managed to keep grunting commands at up to 9g. Under these rigorous circumstances, experimental voice-recognition equipment managed an impressive 90 per cent success rate in identifying his spoken commands. The USAF sees the major application of voice-operated cockpits as future night/all-weather single-seat fighters.

Another technique being tested in the AFTI/F-16 is a helmet-mounted sight for target designation. Instead of positioning target-identification cross-hairs by means of a throttle-mounted cursor control, the AFTI pilot need only look at a target in order to acquire it. The pilot aligns the target with a set of 0·5in (12·7mm) long cross-hairs incorporated in the visor of his helmet. He then depresses the 'target designate' button on his sidestick controller. Orientation of the helmet within the cockpit is measured by a magnetic system incorporating a transmitter mounted on the

canopy immediately behind the pilot's head, and a 4oz (113gm) receiver system on the helmet; the radar or FLIR is automatically slewed to achieve lock-on. Final adjustment is carried out using the cursor controller or by voice command via the VCID system.

If the aircraft systems have detected a target, the location of the latter may be passed to the pilot via the helmet-mounted sight. In this case, miniature lamps at the tips of the visor cross-hairs indicate to the pilot the direction in which he must move his head to acquire the target. When all four are illuminated, the target is in the centre of the cross-hairs.

Flight control system
Probably the boldest step in the original YF-16 design was the decision to adopt an all-electronic fly-by-wire (FBW) flight-control system, instead of the traditional pattern of hydromechanical system with linkages and cables. This was a high-authority command and stability-augmentation system of quadruplexed (four-channel) analogue type, and this configuration was retained for the production aircraft. The weight reductions resulting from the elimination of a mechanical system could be used to allow the large-scale use of fail-safe and fail-operative design techniques, ensuring the high reliability of the electronic equipment.

When details of the F-16 system were first published, they caused some mis-

givings at Saab-Scania in Sweden, where design of the JA-37 Viggen flight-control system was in hand, since the Swedes had opted for a quadruplexed digital system. Despite momentary misgivings, the Swedish decision was a correct one – Fighting Falcon was born too soon to embody a quadruplexed digital system. The latter first entered service in 1977 on the Space Shuttle and a year later on the F/A-18 Hornet.

Without the FBW system, the GD designers could not have positioned the aircraft centre of gravity behind the centre of pressure to give a reduced or negative static margin. The resulting inherent instability is controlled by the FBW system, making the aircraft easy to fly, but gives the controls a high response rate and allows the use of relatively modest amounts of tail deflection during high-g manoeuvres or supersonic flight. During the design of the YF-16, GD engineers estimated that the consequent reduction of trim drag allowed 400lb (181kg) to be shaved off the mission weight of the aircraft.

Lifting tail
The use of relaxed stability also allowed the size of the tail to be reduced, as less force was needed to alter aircraft attitude. Since the tail effectively pushes the rear of the aircraft upwards in order to maintain level flight (the tail on a conventional aircraft pushes downwards), tail trimming forces increase the overall lift.

This diagram illustrates an automated manoeuvring attack by the AFTI/F-16. During the initial run-in (1) the pilot engages the attack system, then carries out a pop-up

FBW systems have been test-flown since the late 1960s, and a rudimentary single-channel analogue system even flew as long ago as 1952 aboard a Tay-engined Viscount airliner testbed. The Panavia Tornado was the first production design to adopt FBW, but this aircraft retained a mechanical backup. The GD team was the first to take the step of eliminating mechanical backups, trusting the safety of the aircraft completely to electronics. Mechanical back-ups were also eliminated on the later F/A-18 Hornet, Mirage 2000 and JA-37 Viggen designs, but Fighting Falcon showed the way. For this reason alone, the GD warplane is assured of a place in aviation history.

For the AFTI/F-16, a full-authority triplex digital flight-control system is used. This is designed to be fault tolerant, so that no single fault should affect correct operation. In the event of a second fault developing, the system is able to revert to a standby condition which will permit safe flight to continue, allowing the aircraft to return to base in such an emergency.

Failures resulting in complete loss of control will be rare, the AFTI specification calling for not more than one per 10 million flight hours. To guard against

manoeuvre (2) to acquire the target and command lock-on. After a period of jinking flight (3) he updates the lock-on (4), then gives the system permission for weapon release (5).

unforeseen failure modes the system incorporates a simple analogue backup flight-control system. Designated the Independent Backup (IBU), this will allow control to be maintained should some drastic failure result in the digital flight-control system being unable to maintain control.

The use of a triplex digital system on the AFTI/F-16 gave GD the confidence to abandon the proven analogue FBW system when creating the Block 25 F-16C/D version of the Fighting Falcon.

In the years since the YF-16 was developed, several US aerospace programmes had expored digital FBW. Triplex (three-channel) digital systems were flight tested in 1976 aboard the Boeing YC-14 and a NASA F-8 testbed, but first US production digital FBW system was the quadruplex (four-channel) equipment on the US Space Shuttle. First US fighter application was the F-18 Hornet, but like Sweden's JA-37 Viggen, this retained mechanical back-up flight controls.

Since the F-16 has no mechanical back-up flight controls, a high standard of FBW reliability was needed. By the early 1980s, GD was happy that this could be achieved with a quadruplex digital system.

Armament

Ordnance carried by the Fighting Falcon ranges from simple weaponry such as unguided rockets and 20mm cannon shells to nuclear weapons. Air-to-air, air-to-ground and specialized anti-ship missiles, along with laser-guided 'smart' bombs, have all been cleared for service, and the F-16 is already slated to receive the most advanced types of weaponry currently under development, including the 'fire and forget' AMRAAM missile needed to cope with next-generation Soviet fighters. Even using straightforward 'iron' bombs, Fighting Falcon can hit its target with greater accuracy than the F-111.

Despite its age, the General Electric 20mm M61A remains the standard USAF fighter cannon. The Service did attempt to develop a caseless 25mm weapon for the F-15 Eagle, but this project bogged down in technical difficulties, so the 20mm seems destined to soldier on through the 1980s.

The M61A1 may be a proven weapon, but its adoption in the F-16 resulted in some initial problems. Gun firing from the type was temporarily forbidden in September 1979 following two incidents in which this resulted in uncommanded yawing movements. Gun vibration was found to be affecting an accelerometer in the flight-control system, causing it to feed false data to the control computer, which in turn demanded the yaw.

A simple modification insulated the accelerometer from vibration. Ten aircraft were modified, assigned to Hill AFB, and successfully participated in a Red Flag exercise. The modification was then introduced into production aircraft, and all 106 operational F-16s delivered with the original pattern of accelerometer installation were modified during 1980.

In its F-16A/B form, the Fighting Falcon was armed with AIM-9 Sidewinder missiles for air-to-air combat. Today's Sidewinders are greatly improved versions of the primitive weapon which first entered production in the mid-1950s. Early Sidewinders may not have required the full cooperation of the target during air-to-air combat, but were restricted to use in classical tail-chase attacks in good weather.

With the arrival of second- and third-generation seeker heads, Sidewinder matured into an agile 'dogfight' missile. European F-16s were originally scheduled to carry the AIM-9J – a rebuilt and modernized version of the early AIM-9B or -9C – but the US Government eventually agreed to make the AIM-9L available. This is a highly agile weapon with all-new guidance seeker and proximity fuze. A total of at least 16,000 are likely to be built in the US, and a further 9,000 or more by a European manufacturing consortium.

BVR missiles

In Vietnam, the MiG-17 and MiG-21 interceptors which challenged US warplanes were equipped only with cannon or short-range guided missiles. US pilots could opt to engage targets under beyond-visual-range (BVR) conditions using the Raytheon AIM-7 Sparrow, or close in to engage in a dogfight with guns and AIM-9 Sidewinders. By the time the F-16 was entering service in significant numbers, it faced the threat of aircraft such as the MiG-23 armed with AA-7 Apex long-range missiles. To engage these in a Sidewinder-armed F-16 would put the Soviet pilot in the same position as US aircrew had been in over Vietnam.

Without improvements, the Fighting Falcon stood the risk of becoming the late-1980s equivalent of the Japanese Zero – lightweight and agile but seriously under-armed. Romantics might argue otherwise, but the day of the simple fighter was coming to an end. Testifying before Congress in 1980, Undersecretary of Defense for Research and Engineering William J. Perry described the F-16A as "an incomplete airplane". Detailing the need for BVR combat capability, he said that "we kidded ourselves a little bit on the F-16, thinking we were buying an inexpensive airplane".

As originally planned, the APG-66 radar was not intended to have the

Above: 20mm cannon shells are loaded into the magazine of an F-16 at Kunsan Air Base, South Korea. A full load consists of 500 rounds.

capability of handling BVR missiles. What the customer asked for – and Westinghouse delivered – was a multimode set sized for the air-to-air mission but offering the many modes necessary for effective ground attack in the 1980s and beyond.

The definitive solution to the problem was the planned AMRAAM (Advanced Medium-Range Air-to-Air Missile), which was due to enter service in the mid-1980s, but USAF planners considered a number of interim solutions for service in the first half of the 1980s. French missile company Matra could offer a radar-guided version of the R.550 Magic. The US, meanwhile, had already fielded and withdrawn a radar-guided AIM-9C version of Sidewinder and had the technology available to develop an updated version of this as a result of the

Below: The smoke pouring from the F-16 on the target range comes not from the engine but from the 6,000rds/min M61A1 cannon.

Semi-Active Medium Pulse-Repetition-Frequency Seeker Demonstration project carried out at China Lake. Either weapon would have given the F-16 a radar capability, but would have done little to improve the engagement range.

Obvious solutions were the longer-range AIM-7 Sparrow or British Aerospace Sky Flash radar-guided missiles. Although larger than AMRAAM, both missiles could provide the required range but would require modifications to the APG-66 in order to provide target-illumination facilities.

Evaluation of a Sparrow-armed YF-16 was carried out by GD, using company funding, with inert rounds carried on wingtip, underwing and fuselage-mounted pylons. The last location involved the pylon being fitted directly on the undercarriage door, and was used for test firings in November 1977. A test firing of the British Sky Flash missile followed a year later, using pylons in the same location.

The need for interim BVR missiles was questioned by some analysts, who claimed that the problems of target-identification would often inhibit BVR attacks, while the higher cost of the missiles would reduce the amount of live-firing training which would be possible. Adoption of either weapon would have been expensive, and AMRAAM development showed no signs of significant slippage in timescale, so plans for the older missiles were shelved.

AIM-120A AMRAAM

F-16C/D Fighting Falcons are equipped to carry and launch the Hughes AIM-120 AMRAAM. This missile is intended to combine the performance of the AIM-7 Sparrow in an airframe not much larger than that of the AIM-9 Sidewinder. The weapon weighs only 326lb (148kg) at launch, compared with 115–195lb (70–88.5kg) for Sidewinder and 503lb (228kg) for the latest versions of Sparrow. Maximum range is more than 30 miles (48km), and the missile is likely to fly at around Mach 4.

AMRAAM flies the initial portion of its trajectory under the control of a midcourse inertial guidance unit which can be updated if neccessary by the launch aircraft. In the later stages of flight, the missile switches on its high-PRF radar seeker and homes onto the target. Since this seeker uses active radar, it does not require the launch aircraft to carry a target illuminator antenna or to continue to track the target after launch. If the target attempts to protect itself with jamming, AMRAAM's seeker can be set to operate in a medium-PRF home-on-jam mode during the midcourse or terminal stages of flight.

Hughes and Raytheon developed rival AMRAAM designs in the late 1970s. Each contractor was due to fire ten prototype rounds from F-14, F-15

Below: This unconventional door-mounted pylon was used for test firings of the Sky Flash shown here, as well as for Sparrow. No F-16 user has ordered the BAe weapon.

Below: the AIM-9 Sidewinder may be a lightweight missile, but lifting its 172lb (78kg) weight into place on the wingtip launch pylon requires significant muscle power.

Above: As a private venture, GD has test-fired radar-guided AIM-7 Sparrow missiles from the YF-16, though no customer has requested Sparrow armament.

and F-16 test aircraft. Firings started in 1981, but after only six shots Hughes was declared the winner in December of that year.

The company launched its first test round in February, with the first guided shot (from an F-16) following on August 26. The round scored an almost central hit on a QF-102 target, which burst into flames and crashed. The missile did not carry a warhead. In a series of six design-validation flight tests, AMRAAM scored two direct hits, one near-miss well within the lethal radius of the warhead, and three failures. The design has now been modified to take account of the experience gained. Test firings will resume in 1984.

Under a $420-million 50-month contract awarded after the 'shoot-off', Hughes is to build some 100 development missiles, 87 of which will be

launched from F-14, F-15, F-16 and F/A-18 aircraft during a two-year series of development and operational test/evaluation firings. Delivery of production rounds will begin in the second half of 1985.

AMRAAM was nowhere near ready for service when the Multinational Staged Improvement Plan (MSIP) was approved in February 1981, but the associated Engineering Change Proposal ECP350 included changes to the aircraft structure and wiring of the wings to allow the weapon to be retrofitted easily at a later date.

Development of the missile has been protracted, with first deployment slipping from an originally planned mid-1980s, and controversy over unit cost. A programme stretchout in 1985 extended full-scale development by 22 months, and should have lead to

mid-1988 deployment, but within a year this had slipped to 1989.

In the summer of 1986, Congress threatened to cancel the programme unless the US Defense Secretary could certify that the design had finally been completed, met the original specification, and could be produced at a unit cost of no more than $440,000. He duly did so, saving the programme, but the delays continued.

Following failures during flight test in 1989, the decision on full-scale production was postponed until 1990. Tests showed that the problem was due to rounds carried on the fuselage stations of the F-15 being exposed to air spilled over the edges of the inlets when the engines were throttled back.

The AIM-120A AMRAAM was rushed into service in the final stages of the Gulf War, a batch of 52 being delivered to the

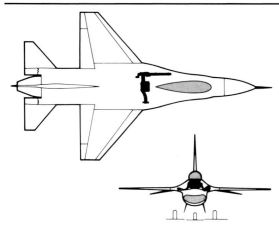

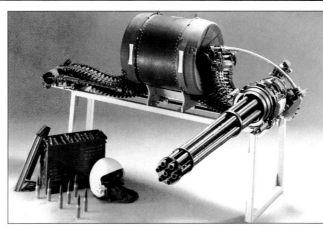

Far left: Location of the M61A1 cannon, ammunition drum and feed in the F-16. GD studies have shown that 30mm DEFA, 27mm Mauser or 30mm Oerlikon KCA could be accommodated should a heavier and more destructive projectile be desired. Left: In creating the M61 series of aircraft cannon, the Armament division of General Electric revived the rotary principle first devised by the legendary Dr Gatling. This involves rotating the entire barrel assembly: while one barrel is firing, the remaining five are at different stages of the loading/unloading cycle. The result is a very high rate of fire and high reliability.

USAF's 58th TFS at Tabuk for use of the F-15C. By this time the Iraqi air force was effectively grounded, so AMRAAM saw no combat.

Although the total buy had been trimmed from 24,320 down to 15,450 to match planned US force reductions, the deployment showed that this long-awaited weapon was finally ready for full-scale production.

AGM-65 Maverick

The six underwing pylons and single under-fuselage hardpoint of the F-16 allow a heavy ordnance load to be carried, including air-to-surface missiles, 'smart' bombs, tactical nuclear weapons and conventional iron bombs. One of the most important warloads of US F-16s will be the Hughes AGM-65 Maverick used for precision attacks against point targets. This is available in AGM-65A, AGM-65B and AGM-65D forms, which use TV guidance, scene-magnification TV guidance and imaging infra-red (IIR) guidance respectively. The last can be used in day, night or adverse-weather conditions. Currently under development are the AGM-65E laser-guided version and AGM-65F IR-guided variants, but these are intended for use by the US Marine Corps and Navy respectively. All versions use common aft and centre sections and have the same aerodynamic configuration.

More than 26,000 TV-guided rounds were built, demonstrating an 86 per cent hit rate in 1,221 firings. Average miss distance during a series of tests against tank-sized targets was only 3ft (0.91m). A vidicon (TV) seeker in the nose of the missile may be slewed upon its two-axis mounting and used to view the target area. Using a TV image on the cockpit display, the pilot can align the target on the aiming mark, then command lock-on.

AGM-65A has a 5deg field of view, while the AGM-65B Scene Magnification variant has a 2.5deg field of view but can detect targets at longer range thanks to the increased image scale. These early-model Mavericks are not ideally suited to use from single-seat fighters due to the time needed to acquire the target and lock-on the missile seeker. Moreover, visibility conditions in many parts of the world can reduce target detection range to the point where the pilot of a high-speed aircraft no longer has time to operate the weapon. This problem has been appreciated for some time, spurring development of the IR-guided AGM-65D.

Imaging infra-red

The operating principle of the IR version is similar to that of the -65A and -65B, but in this case a thermal image is displayed in the cockpit instead of TV. Two magnifications are provided – wide angle for target acquisition, and narrow angle for final identification and lock-on.

The AGM-65D seeker is based on

mechanical scanning, a ring of faceted mirrors rotating at 3,600rpm to focus the IR energy on an array of 16 detectors. More modern seekers have no moving parts, but use a staring array consisting of thousands of individual detectors to cover the entire field of view simultaneously. This technology was not ready when the -65D was developed.

As the aircraft fly out to the target area, the detector elements are precooled for maximum sensitivity. Once a target has been spotted, a protective cover over the seeker dome is jettisoned, allowing the IR system to "see" the terrain, passing this image to a cockpit-mounted head-down CRT screen in the aircraft cockpit.

The seeker is steered manually on to a suitable target, which can be up to 15deg from the nose of the aircraft. Even when using the wide field of view, this manoeuvre has been described as like searching for a target by peering through a drinking straw. During the 1991 Gulf War, F-16 pilots expressed concern at having to fly head-down while locking the narrow field-of-view missile seeker on to the target and releasing the weapon.

At the moment of launch, the aircraft

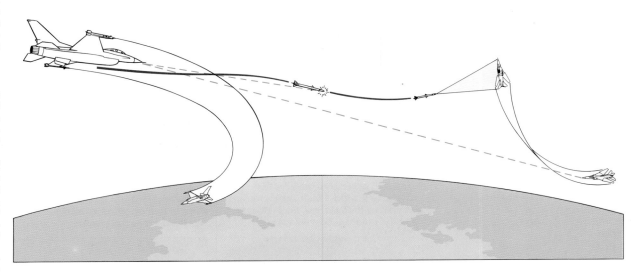

Above: After launching the fire-and-forget AMRAAM missile, the F-16 pilot will be able to turn away. The round will home onto the target during the final stages of flight using an active-radar seeker. Right: Internal arrangement of AMRAAM.

Right: Destruction of a QF-102 drone by the first guided AMRAAM launch.

Below right: Internal arrangement of the TV-guided Maverick.

Below: Maximum range and height of Maverick launching have been declassified following the export.

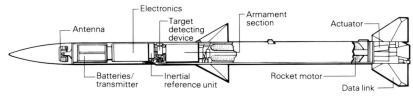

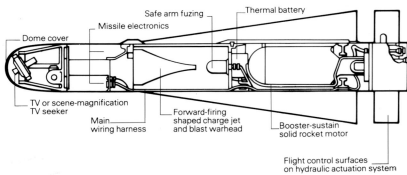

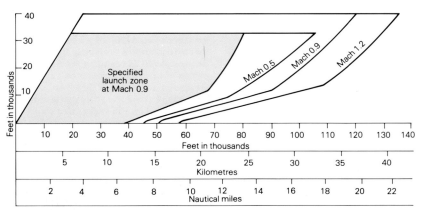

The first full-scale development F-16B releases a Maverick in a diving attack. An operational launch at such altitudes would require massive ECM protection for the aircraft.

must be flying in a stable manner. The brief first burn of the Thiokol rocket motor takes the round off the launch rail; the second lasts for five seconds, boosting the missile to a top speed of Mach 2. One difference is that Maverick operations normally involve using the missile seeker to locate the target: with the IIR version, the seeker may be slaved to or cued by target-acquisition systems such as Pave Penny or LANTIRN.

After launch, the round flies a proportional-navigation course, cruising under the impulse given by a solid-propellant rocket motor. All versions of Maverick have roughly the same launch zone. The missile can be launched at dive angles of up to 60deg, while maximum launch altitude varies according to aircraft speed, and generally lies between 33,000 and 40,000ft (10,000–12,000m). Above this height the round would become aerodynamically unstable.

Maximum range varies according to aircraft speed and height – from more than 22nm (25 miles/41km) at Mach 1.2/40,000ft down to around 7nm (8 miles/13km) at Mach 0.5 at low level. At lower altitudes, maximum range is dictated by the loss of kinetic energy during the coasting stage of flight. Above 10,000ft (3,000m) or so, endurance of the thermal batteries used to provide on-board electrical power is the limiting factor. There is no minimum launch altitude, but the minimum launch range is constrained by the limitations of the guidance and the need for the launch aircraft to avoid the exploding warhead.

The warhead is a 125lb (57kg) shaped charge unit with good secondary blast effects, and is effective against a wide range of tactical targets including moving or stationary armoured vehicles and trucks; artillery; SAM systems and their associated radars; and aircraft parked in revetments or hardened shelters. The warhead is located aft of the seeker, but the latter incorporates a

Above: 1,000lb (454kg) iron bombs are released from the first F-16XL.

Top right: Two-seat F-16/79 launches a Paveway laser-guided bomb.

'tunnel' to allow the gas jet from the charge to pass freely. (An alternative penetrator/blast-fragment warhead developed for the USN and USMC versions is fitted with selectable fuzing so that it can be set to detonate either on initial impact with the target, or after penetration.)

Maverick requires little modification of the parent aircraft, and can be carried on the three-round LAU-88/A and LAU-88A/A launchers or the single-rail LAU-117/A. A modified version of the LAU-88/A with drag-reducing fairings, including a 'boat-tail' aft section, is intended for use on high-performance aircraft such as the F-16. Drag is reduced by some 45–60 per cent depending on flight profile. Mavericks can be loaded on to the launcher and go/no-go tested as a complete assembly.

Modifications to the LAU-88/A have been devised to allow rapid fire against multiple targets. The modified launcher contains facilities for: ground boresighting all missiles to the 'pipper' of the aircraft sighting system; operating two missiles at the same time, with the seeker head of the second slaved to that of the first; holding the aim of the second round after the launch of the first; and providing a safe time interval between dome cover ejection and missile launch.

One Maverick tactic tested during AGM-65D trials during 1982 involved the use of an F-16 and an F-111 working as a 'hunter-killer' team. Using a belly-mounted AVQ-26 Pave Tack FLIR pod, an F-111F was able to locate and designate a ground target, then use a voice link to call in the Maverick-armed F-16.

In August 1978 one of the YF-16s became the first single-seat aircraft to deliver smart bombs without assistance

Above: The F-16/79 releases iron bombs over a US range. European air arms have long since abandoned medium altitude dive attacks, but the USAF has great faith in ECM.

from a second target-designating aircraft during a series of 46 industry-sponsored test flights carried out in 1978. For these tests, the aircraft carried a Martin Marietta/Thomson-CSF Atlis pod under the intake.

Developed by Martin Marietta and the French company Thomson-CSF, Atlis (Automatic-Tracking Laser Illumination System) is a pod-mounted system consisting of a stabilized TV system able to lock on to targets selected by the pilot, and a target-designation laser able to 'mark' targets during missile or smart bomb attacks. It allows the aircraft to break away immediately after missile launch in order to avoid being engaged by enemy point-defence systems. During the first trial, the aircraft delivered a GBU-10 bomb from an altitude of 5,000ft (1,524m), entering a 4g turn immediately after weapon release.

Other missiles

Some export operators carry their own specialised air-to-air and air-to-surface weapons on the F-16. The most common air-to-air missile remains the AIM-9 Sidewinder, but not all users are cleared to receive the AIM-9L. The alternative is to use export-model Sidewinders such as the AIM-9P3 or the newer all-aspect -9P4 – or else buy non-US missiles. Several have chosen the latter course.

Qualification firings of the Matra R.550 Magic 2 missile from the F-16 began in May 1989.

The same year also saw the successful integration of the Rafael Python 3 missile on the F-16. An adaptor allows the Israeli missile to fit on to Sidewinder launch rails. A follow-on to the earlier Shafrir, Python was rushed into service during the 1982 Israeli invasion of Lebanon, with

Right: 388th TFW Fighting Falcons set course on a training mission.

Below right: Penguin anti-ship missile under the wing of an RNoAF F-16.

pre-production rounds being tested in air combat against the Syrian Air Force. It will be followed into service by the further-improved Python 4.

With the F16 set to serve well into the next century, users and weapon manufacturers alike are exploring new weapon fits and even new weapons which would keep the aircraft combat effective. Teaming the aircraft with an off-the-shelf missile can be a particularly cost-effective solution.

Sparrow can provide the F-16 with a degree of beyond-visual-range (BVR) capability without the high cost and export restrictions associated with AMRAAM. First test-firing of Sparrow from an F-16C came in May 1989, and followed an earlier trial using an F-16A.

First export customer to fit Sparrow to an F-16 was Bahrain, which took delivery of its first F-16C and D aircraft in 1990. Second was Egypt, which specified the weapon for 41 F-16C/D aircraft ordered in November 1987 under the Peace Vector III programme. Sparrow also arms the F-16A/B Air Defence Fighter interceptors of the US Air National Guard.

The new Active Skyflash being developed by BAe could prove an attractive alternative to AMRAAM for foreign F-16 operators not cleared by the US Government to receive the US missile. This fire-and-forget weapon combines the fuselage, motor and warhead of the existing Skyflash with a new pattern of active-radar seeker developed for the missile by Thomson-CSF.

In the long term, NATO had planned to replace the Sidewinder with the collaboratively developed AIM-132 ASRAAM (Advanced Short Range Air to Air Missile), but West Germany's decision in 1989 to abandon the programme has

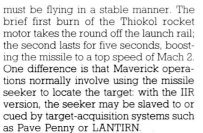

created a problem for its partners, who must try to find new industrial partners. It was less important for the USA, whose interest in the programme had been lukewarm at best. The US was working on the improved AIM-9R version of Sidewinder, and had already investigated alternative seekers for future upgrades.

Such "Super Sidewinders" are expected to serve with the USAF until around the late 1990s. For service beyond the year 2000, the US is looking at new heat-seeking missiles, perhaps of conformal shape intended as "scab-on" armament for stealthy aircraft such as the F-22 Advanced Tactical Fighter. Matra's MICA remains a possible armament for export F-16s, particularly in the MICAS-RAAAM version proposed in 1990 as a possible alternative to ASRAAM.

Improvements to the internal gun are limited to a new longer-ranged ammunition currently under development, although the Block 40 modifications introduced an improved gunsight (see Avionics chapter). The New York ANG beefed up the firepower of its F-16s by adding a pod-mounted GPU-5 30mm cannon. This fires the same cartridge as the A-10's GAU-8 gun, and has a maximum rate of fire of 2,400 rounds/min. A cockpit switch allows the pilot to select the internal 20mm gun, the gun pod, or both.

In 1990, the USAF collaborated with McDonnell Douglas to integrate the AGM-88 version of the Harpoon anti-ship missile on the F-16C/D. Bahrain was reported to be interested in fitting the weapon to its F-16s.

A major boost in firepower could be added to the F-16 by a new Low-Cost Advanced Technology Missile (LOCATM) being studied by Martin Marietta, McDonnell Douglas and Rockwell International. Instead of a normal armament such as six AGM-65 Maver-

icks or six Mk 82 bombs, the aircraft would carry two Expendable Intelligent Multiple Ejector Rack (XIMER) units, each containing two three-round bays for LOCATM rounds.

The drag of two XIMER would be lower than that of six Mavericks or bombs, increasing aircraft range and speed. Maximum range of LOCATM would be higher than that of Maverick, perhaps as much as 25 miles (40km).

XIMER units

XIMER units would be fitted with their missiles at the factory, then tested, sealed, and delivered to the customer as a "wooden round" which can be stored for up to 15 – 20 years, then fitted to the aircraft without further testing. Projected cost of an XIMER and its six missiles is around $200,000.

The round would be powered either by three individual 2.75in (7cm) diameter rocket motors or by a single three-pulse design. Launched from beyond visual range, LOCATM would navigate using a GPS satnav receiver, switching to a millimetre-wave of IR seeker for the final moments of target detection and homing.

Little is known about the Northrop AGM-137 Tri-Service Standoff Attack Missile planned for service on the F-15, F-16, F/A-18, A-6, B-52, and B-2. Designed to carry a single warhead or a payload of submunitions against high-value land or naval targets, this stealthy cruise long-range cruise missile has been under development since 1986. The weapon is subsonic, weighs around 2,300lb (1,040kg) and will have a range of less than 370 miles (600km) when air launched, falling to less than 310 miles for the proposed AGM-137 land-launched version. The latter will be fired from the Army's MLRS launch vehicle. A total of 8,650 rounds are to be built.

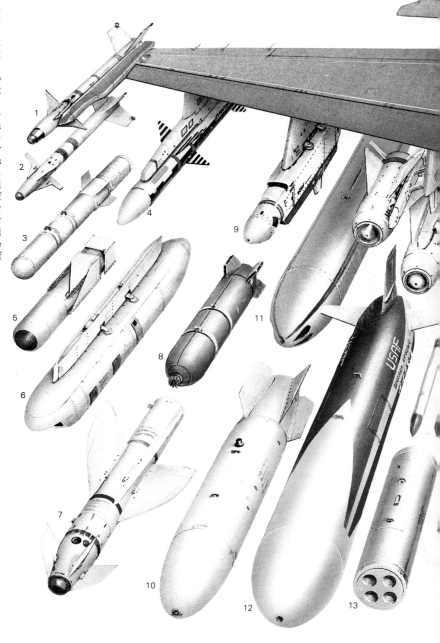

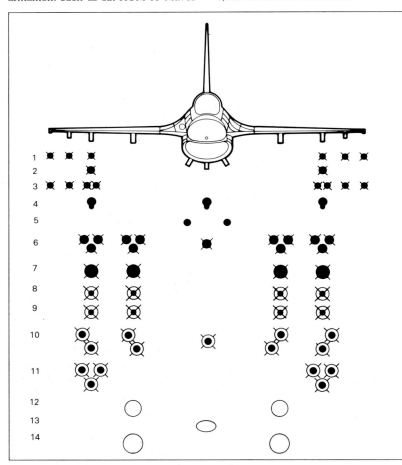

USAF F-16 stores loadings:
1: AIM-9 Sidewinder. 2: AIM-7 Sparrow (proposed). 3: AIM-120 AMRAAM. 4: ALQ-131 ECM pods. 5: Electro-optical/infra-red/terrain-following radar pods. 6: Up to 25 Mk 82 1,000lb (454kg) bombs. 7: Mk 84 **2,000lb (907kg) bombs. 8: and 9: Paveway or GBU-15 laser-guided bombs. 10: Up to 17 cluster bombs. 11: AGM-45 Maverick. 12: 370gal fuel tanks. 13: 300gal fuel tank. 14: 600gal fuel tanks.**

1 AIM-9L Sidewinder
2 AIM-9J Sidewinder
3 Durandal anti-runway weapon
4 AIM-120 AMRAAM
5 Wasp air-to-surface mini-missile (proposed)
6 Orpheus recce pod (RNethAF only)
7 Penguin Mk 3 anti-ship missile
8 Cluster munition
9 ALQ-131 ECM pod
10 Nuclear bomb
11 GEPOD 30mm gun pod
12 AGM-109 MRASM cruise missile (proposed)
13 SUU-25 flare
14 TV or IIR-guided AGM-45 Maverick
15 SUU-20 practice carrier
16 LAU rocket launcher
17/18 proposed electro-optical, FLIR and radar pods

19 ATLIS II designator pod (trials only)
20 Paveway laser-guided bomb
21 Mk 82 500lb (227kg) general-purpose bombs
22 HOBO 'smart' bomb
23 Mk 84 2,000lb (907kg) general-purpose bomb
24 Mk 82 Snakeye retarded bomb
25 External fuel tank
26 AGM-78 Standard ARM anti-radar missile
27 Mk 83 1,000lb (454kg) bomb
28 Mk 117 750lb (340kg) bomb
29 AGM-45A Shrike anti-radar missile
30 AGM-88 HARM anti-radar missile
31 Radar-detection pod (for proposed Wild Weasel two-seater)

Left: Even with simple iron bombs, the F-16 offers exceptionally accurate delivery. During some trials, diameter of the weapon impact area was only one third of the specified figure.

Right: During low-altitude attacks, the tail fins of the Snakeye 500lb (227kg) bomb open to retard the weapon. The impact point is thus well to the rear of the aircraft, protecting it from blast and debris.

Above: The impressive array of stores carried by, tested on or designed to be compatible with the Fighting Falcon belies the type's original conception as a cheap and simple lightweight fighter.

Right: USAF technicians check 500lb (227kg) bombs on a munition cart, prior to loading them aboard an F-16 during exercise Cope Elite 81. As a result of MSIP modifications, all hardpoints are likely to be cleared to a 9g load factor.

Combat and Deployment

Ordered by the USAF, adopted by four NATO air arms and high on the shopping list of the Imperial Iranian Air Force, the F-16 was never far from the headlines in the late 1970s. With three production lines tooled up, aircraft were delivered in ever-increasing numbers, and other air forces joined the queue to take delivery of General Dynamics' latest creation: by 1990 Fighting Falcon had already been ordered by 18 nations on five of the seven continents. This number is certain to be exceeded as the result of further export sales and the supply of ex-USAF "hand-me-down" aircraft to US allies.

The USAF accepted its first production F-16 on August 17, 1978, and the first delivery to an operational unit followed on January 6, 1979. First unit to be equipped was the 388th Tactical Fighter Wing at Hill AFB, Utah, which built up to its full strength of 102 Fighting Falcons by the end of 1980, and trained aircrew for TAC and export customers.

In the hands of 388th TFW pilots, the Fighting Falcon began to show its mettle. Three days of war games held at Hill AFB in March 1980 showed how the aircraft could be used to reinforce the NATO Central Front or any other trouble spot. Refuelling from KC-135 tankers, 12 aircraft carried out a 7,000km (4,350-mile) transit flight lasting 10 hours to simulate overseas deployment, followed by two days of intensive flying.

Despite the sophistication of the new warplane and its avionic systems, the care taken during design and development to ensure reliability and easy

Below: A heavily-armed F-16C operated by the 363rd TFW heads north to attack Iraqi targets during the Gulf War.

maintenance paid off from the beginning, and unit after unit converting to the type found itself clocking up flying hours at a higher-than-predicted rate. In 1979 the average number of hardware failures per flight hour for USAF aircraft was around 1·2, against an eventual goal of only 0·34. During the second half of 1979 the actual failure rate of the F-16s at Hill AFB varied from just under 1·2 down to around 0·75, and this showed signs of falling to the target figure by the early 1980s.

By 1980 the F-16 was displaying impressive reliability in the field. Tactical Air Command standard for mission capability is 70 per cent, but by 1980 the Fighting Falcon was averaging 74 to 76 per cent, making it the most reliable fighter in the US inventory. Both figures quoted refer to the number of aircraft completely or partly mission capable.

Fighting Falcon officially started its operational career with the USAF on November 12, 1980, when the 4th Tactical Fighter Squadron – part of the 388th TFW – achieved Initial Operational Capability. In March of the following year this unit took 12 Fighting Falcons

overseas for the first time during a month-long deployment to Flesland in Norway. If further proof were needed that the Fighting Falcon was a success, this was provided in June 1981 when seven 388th TFW aircraft won the Royal Air Force-sponsored tactical bombing competition held at Lossiemouth in Scotland, defeating RAF Jaguars and Buccaneers and USAF F-111Es.

By the spring of 1982, the USAF fleet had exceeded 100,000 flying hours. A total of 345 was in service at that time with TAC operational units.

Deployment of the Fighting Falcon to the USAFE's 17th Air Force in what was then West Germany started in December 1982. After a period of initial training at Zaragoza in Spain, the 50th TWF's 313rd Tactical Fighter Squadron became operational at Hahn, followed by the 496th and 10th TFS. Three more squadrons – the 417th, 512th, and 526th from the 86th TFW at Ramstein also switched to the F-16.

Re-equipment of the 16th Air Force's 401st TFW at Torrejon in Spain started in 1983. The wing's 612th, 613rd & 614th AFS were due to move to Crotone in Italy in

Above: On its way to the Gulf, an F-16 closes with its refueling tanker. Such operations became commonplace during the 1991 Gulf War.

1991, but shortage of funding may delay this.

Production of the F-16A and B for the USAF ended in the winter of 1984/5, and all but 50 or so of the 785 delivered to the USAF were still in service at the end of the decade. Production of the first (Block 25) F-16C and D models started in 1984.

F-16s replaced the older F-4 Phantom, gradually becoming the USAF's main ground attack aircraft. 1987 saw the 52nd TFW at Spangdahlem begin to deploy the Block 30 F-16C/D as a replacement for its F-4Es. The base houses the 23rd, 81st and 480th TFS, who flew a mixed fleet of F-4G Wild Weasel Phantoms.

The first Fighting Falcons deployed to Europe were Block 15 production standard, with the larger horizontal tail surfaces, and inlet hardpoints for AMRAAM missiles and LANTIRN sensors. By 1989 the USAFE had traded all of its F-16A/B aircraft for the newer C/D models, night operations using LANTIRN having started in West Germany late that year.

By the end of the 1980s, around 1,500 had been delivered, and production had switched to the Block 40/42 version.

F-16s also serve in the Pacific. First deliveries to the 8th TFW at Kunsan in South Korea were in 1981, ahead of deliveries to the USAFE in Germany. The Pacific Air Force currently consists of the 5th Air Force in Japan, the 7th in South Korea, the 11th in Alaska, and the 13th in the Philippines. The 5th AF's 432nd TFW has two F-16 units, the 13th and 14th TFS, both based at Misawa AB, Japan. The 7th AF in South Korea initially had the 8th TFW at Kunsan AB (35th & 80th TFS), but these were supplemented in the late 1980s by the 51st TFW, which now operates two F-16 squadrons.

The 11th AF has no F-16s, but some serve in the aggressor role with the 13th Air Force's 3rd TFW at Clark AFB in the Philippines. Twelve F-16s also serve with the 527th Aggressor Squadron at RAF Bentwaters in the UK, part of the 3rd Air Force.

In the mid-1980s, the F-16 and Northrop's private-venture F-20 Tigershark were evaluated against the Air Defense Fighter (ADF) requirement to re-equip ANG interceptor units. The decision in October 1986 to adopt a modified F-16A spelled the end of Tigershark, but resulted in several F-16A/B fighters being rebuilt for the interceptor role, and re-armed with Sparrow missiles.

The first rebuilt aircraft was delivered in early 1989. First unit to deploy the rebuilt aircraft was the 114th Tactical Fighter Training Squadron of the Oregon ANG, followed shortly afterwards by the 194th Fighter Interceptor Squadron of the California ANG.

Although smaller than the F-4, the F-16 ADF has a longer range, and better capability against low-signature targets such as cruise missiles, and the light aircraft often used for drug-running flights.

The F-15 ADF will equip a total of 10 squadrons, a mixture of Air Force and Air National Guard units. Most were due to have re-equipped by 1992.

The 26 F-16N aircraft built for the Navy in 1987/88 are used for dissimilar air combat training. These F-16N are based on the standard F-16C/D and are powered by the GE F110-GE-100 engine. The aircraft have a strengthened wing, and are able to carry Air Combat Manoeuvring Instrumentation (ACMI). Despite being F-16C airframes, the F-16Ns retain the APG-66 radar used in the F-16A. They have no cannon or ASPJ; their EW fit consists of an ALR-69 RWR and the ALE-40 chaff/flare dispenser.

Initial order was for 22 single-seater and four two-seat trainers. IOC was in April 1987 at Naval Air Station Miramar, with NAS Key West being equipped in October of the same year. The F-16N equips the Naval Fighter Weapons School (Top Gun), also VF-45 and VF-126. Deliveries ended in May 1988.

Kuwait 1990

With the gradual thaw in East/West political tension in the late 1980s and the ending of the Cold War, it began to seem possible that the USAF's Fighting Falcons might one day retire without ever having seen a shot fired in anger. When the Iraqi Army poured over the border with Kuwait in August 1990, to begin the annexation of that nation, they set in motion a military build-up by the US and an ever-growing number of allies.

As part of the build-up, a force of 24 F-16s made the longest Fighting Falcon flight to date, taking off from the US at sunset, flying east through the night, and seeing sunrise when close to Gibraltar. The aircraft flew on through that day, finally touching down in Saudi Arabia just before sunset. A total of ten in-flight refuellings was needed, and all the aircraft arrived together. Eight days after the invasion of Kuwait, the Fighting Falcon was ready for action.

ANG F-16 units served alongside their USAF counterparts, learning new skills such as use of the ALQ-119 jamming pod. Although in the ANG inventory, the elderly ALQ-119-15 pod was not normally issued to the squadrons. Pod failure rate was high at first, until maintenance crews and pilots mastered the system.

Most of the F-16s sent to the Gulf were Block 40 models. By now, testing at Edwards AFB had allowed restrictions imposed when the aircraft first entered service to be relaxed. These had limited extreme manoeuvres when certain external stores were carried.

With the US and its allies determined to make the best use of Western nightfighting capability, most F-16s were fitted with LANTIRN navigation pods. The targeting pods were still in short supply. Priority was given to the F-15E force, so few were available for use on the F-16.

F-16s of the USAF and ANG took part in the opening air strikes on the night of January 16th/17th. The defences on that first day of the air war were as heavy as those experienced in Vietnam two decades earlier. One squadron reported the firing of around 80 SAMs against it, but within days the main threat had fallen to AAA and small-arms fire.

The F-16 played a major role in the air

Above: An F-16N and A4 in formation, both with the markings of aggressor units. Twenty-six F-16s were built to fulfil this role for the Navy.

campaign, attacking a wide range of targets, including fixed sites, radar systems, and both moving and dug-in tanks and other vehicles. Typical weapons used were a pair of Mk 84 bombs, six Mk 82 bombs, CBU-52 and -58 cluster munitions, the CBU-87 Combined Effects Munition, and the AIM-65 Maverick.

By the time the ground war began, many F-16 pilots had 100 hours or more of combat flight time. Using the aircraft's CCIP aiming mode, pilots managed CEPs of 30-40ft (9-12m) with iron bombs – a fifth of that achieved during the Vietnam War – while still being free to choose the best flight path for avoiding defensive fire.

Maverick was to see significant combat use, the infra-red seeker of the AGM-65D proving ideal in the dry desert conditions. A smaller number of the older AGM-65A/B TV-guided version were also used.

Kill rate in combat was about 80 per cent. "Wherever you aim the Maverick, it hits the target," one ANG pilot told the US magazine *Aviation Week and Space Technology* as the ground war to liberate Kuwait got under way in February.

Maverick is expensive, so was kept for high-value targets such as tanks. As the Iraqi armour remained dug in for most of the war, opportunities to use the weapon were not as common as pilots had hoped. By mid-February, Iraqi armour was beginning to move in attempts to disperse. As the USAF sought to inflict maximum attrition on the Iraqi forces before the ground forces moved in, 100 or more rounds were being fired per day. One post-war estimate suggested that as many as 5,000 were fired in combat during the month-long war.

With the Iraqi air force largely knocked out in the opening days of the war, or forced to flee to Iran, the Fighting Falcons were denied the chance to take on the MiG-29 or any other Iraqi fighters. The small number of Iraqi aircraft downed in air-to-air combat all fell to F-15 Eagles.

Long hours of air patrol did prove that the long-awaited Hughes AIM-120A AMRAAM was a mature design. Only two rounds of the rounds rushed to the Gulf failed during around 2,600 hours of combat service on the F-15.

Force reductions planned for the early 1990s will see older types such as the F-4 and A-7 retired. The F-16 will eventually make up 40 per cent of the tactical fighter force, sharing the close-support and battlefield interdiction task with the A-10. Ideally the F-16 would handle all close-support missions, leaving the A-10 to act as a forward air controller, but shortage of funds plus the A-10's success in the 1991 Gulf War will keep the subsonic aircraft in service.

With the USAFE's F-14G Wild Weasels due for retirement in the early 1990s, the associated F-16s will switch from the anti-radar task back to ground attack.

From 1993 onwards, the pod-equipped RF-16C is due to replace the RF-4C.

By the time that F-16 production for the USAF ends, the service hopes to have taken delivery of around 2,700 Fighting Falcons. By late 1990 funding had been allocated for a total of more than 2,000.

Like all Western defence plans, these figures are likely to be reduced by defence cuts. Under the US defence budget announced in early 1991, production of the F-16 would fall from 108 aircraft in fiscal year 1991 to 48 in 1991, and a final buy of 24 in 1993. If not supported by foreign orders, the line would then close.

Below: Taxiying in at the end of another successful sortie over Iraq, this F-16C carries a centreline ALQ-119 ECM pod.

Above: An F-16 of the Royal Netherlands Air Force. The RNAF began converting to F-16s from F-104Gs in June 1979.

The Force Aérienne Belge/Belgische Luchtmarcht (Belgian Air Force) was the first European operator to take delivery of locally-built Fighting Falcons. The original Belgian order was for 116 aircraft – 96 single-seaters and 20 two-seat trainers – and the first example was accepted on January 29, 1979.

On January 16, 1981, 349 Sqn of the FAéB was officially assigned to NATO, and on May 6 it was declared fully operational. Belgium will deploy three F-16 wings. No 1 Wing at Beauvechain consists of two squadrons – 349 and 350 – each with 32 aircraft. The latter squadron was the second FAéB unit to convert to the type. 10 Wing at Kleine-Brogel consists of 23 and 31 Squadrons. As F-16 conversion continued, the MTU was transferred from Beauvechain to Klein

Brogel. Once conversion is completed it will disband, and key staff will move to the FAéB Technical School at Saffraanberg.

Within two years of taking delivery of its first F-16As the Belgian Air Force reported an availability rate of 88 per cent. Mean time between failures was 2.9 hours, while the 12 man-hours of maintenance required per flying hour was well below that of many earlier types. Turnaround time was between 15 and 45 minutes, depending on the type of mission being flown.

The Belgian Air Force was the first to use the Fighting Falcon in the somewhat unwarlike role of target tug. Tests carried out at Solenzara in Corsica using a No 1 Wing aircraft tested various underwing and fuselage locations for the pods associated with Tetraplan and Secapem B90 targets, as well as the newer Taxan design which incorporates an acoustic scoring system. These tests included jettison trials in which an Alpha Jet was

used as photographic chase plane.

Delivery of the first 116 aircraft was completed in May 1985. Tactical Air Force Command then had six squadrons of Fighting Falcons – 1, 2, 23, 31, 349 and 350, plus an OCU.

A follow-on batch of 44 Block 15 OCU aircraft was delivered between 1987 and 1991, allowing retirement of some of Belgium's elderly Mirage VBR. The Dassault aircraft had been in service since the early 1970s, serving with two wings, but by the mid-1980s attrition had reduced the fleet from the original 88 to around 70. Most are being retired, but 20 are being upgraded, and will serve until 2005.

Update planned

Under present plans, Belgium is committed to giving its Fighting Falcons a mid-life update which will help them serve into the early years of the next century. The aircraft will also be fitted with the Carapace passive EW system,

and new air-to-surface munitions.

Belgium did consider joining the planned Agile Falcon programme (see final chapter for details of this variant), but was reluctant to commit itself to purchasing the aircraft. Plans to purchase new fighters such as EFA or Rafale were shelved in April 1989, and an order is unlikely to be placed until after 2000.

Beginning in September 1981, a total of 35 early-production Belgian Air Force F-16s were rotated back through the SABCA factory at Gosselies in Belgium for cockpit modifications and updating of the avionics, including the APG-66 radar. This work followed the completion of intensive operational evaluation of the aircraft.

At the same time, the Rapport III ECM system was installed internally. This involves rewiring the aircraft, and since only a few technicians can work within the confined space of the cockpit and nose section at any one time, the work is slow. Each aircraft spends about six months at the factory, and the modified Falcons are delivered back to the user at a rate of around one a month. At this build standard they are known as Block 10 aircraft. The same factory continues with new production work, Belgian aircraft from the 54th onwards being built to the revised standard.

Deliveries of F-16 aircraft to the Kongelige Danske Flyvevåbnet (Royal Danish Air Force) started on January 28, 1980. The current order is for 46 single-seat F-16A fighters plus 12 two-seat F-16B trainers, and the first squadrons to convert were Esk 727 and 730 at Skrystrup. The former unit was declared operational to NATO on August 26, 1981. Four Danish instructors were trained at Hill AFB, and assigned to Esk 727.

Final two squadrons to equip with Fighting Falcon were Esk 723 and 726 at Ålborg. With the four squadrons flying the F-16, Denmark was able to phase out older aircraft such as the F-104G Starfighter, and the F-100 Super Sabre.

A follow-on batch of 12 Block 15 OCU aircraft (eight single-seat and four two-seater) was ordered in 1985 for delivery

Left: In 1980, soon after the delivery of the Dutch F-16s, the Royal Norwegian Air Force took delivery of their first aircraft.

Above: Norwegian airfields are snow-covered for much of the year, a factor which caused the RNoAF to request braking parachutes in its F-16s.

in 1989. There are attrition replacements; new aircraft will still have to be found in the 1990s to re-equip Esk 725 and 729.

Both squadrons currently fly a modernised version of the J35 Draken in the fighter, recce and training roles. These aircraft are the updated survivors of 51 Drakens purchased in 1968. Fighting Falcon would be a logical replacement, but plans to buy new aircraft for these units could fall victim to east-west defence cuts.

The 1975 agreement between the United States and the four European F-16 operators covered work on 998 aircraft – 348 for the European air arms and 650 for the USAF. This workload tailed off, but the US offered further work in return for F-16 follow-on orders being placed in 1983. The first aircraft of the Belgian follow-on order of 44 F-16s was delivered in 1987, to replace their Dassault-Mirage 5BRs.

Rather than operate 'twinned' squadrons, the Koninklijke Luchtmacht (Royal Netherlands Air Force) opted to shut down each of the units converting to the Fighting Falcon for the year or so that the transition required. The first F-16 was accepted on June 6, 1979, an operational conversion unit having been set up at Leeuwarden, home base of 322 Sqn, the first to convert from the F-104G. The first instructors were trained at Hill AFB in the USA. Local pilot and crew training started at Leeuwarden in October 1979, and the first newly-converted pilot joined 322 Sqn in December of the same year.

322 Sqn completed conversion by the end of April 1981. 323 Sqn (also based at Leeuwarden) was the next to be stood down to begin conversion to the Fighting Falcon. A second OCU was set up at Volkel, home base of 306, 311 and 312 Sqns to tackle the conversion of these units, a task which started in 1982.

Right: The immaculate condition of this Danish Air Force F-16A, its hangar, mobile tool kit and work platforms would satisfy the most fastidious inspecting officer.

Fighting Falcon in the KLu

Like all European F-16 operators, the KLu uses the Fighting Falcon primarily in the close support role. In addition to carrying out air-to-ground attacks, Dutch F-16s are also used as air-superiority fighters both in the battle area and in the air-defence region allocated to the KLu by NATO.

The last squadron to convert, Nr 306, formerly flew the RF-104G reconnaissance aircraft. When re-equipped with Fighting Falcon, it will continue to specialise in reconnaissance, carrying the Oldelft Orpheus recce pod. This role requires only minor adaption of the F-16. Originally deployed on the Starfighter, the Orpheus pod carries five cameras and an infra-red line scanner.

In March 1980 the Netherlands announced plans to increase its F-16 fleet from 102 aircraft (80 F-16A and 22 F-16B) to 213, but the only follow-on announced by the summer of 1983 was

for 22 aircraft intended to act as attrition replacements.

Delivery of 60 F-16A and 12 F-16B aircraft to the Kongelige Norske Luftforsvaret (Royal Norwegian Air Force) started on January 25, 1980, and four squadrons will operate the type by 1984. Like its NATO partners, the RNoAF sent an initial batch of personnel to Hill AFB for training. On their return to Norway, these instructors were assigned to Skv 332, Norway's first Fighting Falcon unit, for conversion training. By the autumn of 1981, Skv 332 was fully equipped with F-16s and Skv 331 – the first operational unit – had already received many of its aircraft.

Skv 331 and 332 are based at Bodo, and formerly flew F-104G Starfighters. They were followed through the conversion process by Skv 338 from Norland (a former F-5 unit) and Skv 334 from Bodo (formerly an anti-shipping unit whose CF-104D/G fighters were armed with Bullpup missiles). For attacks against

surface vessels, RNoAF F-16s are equipped with the indigenously developed Penguin Mk 3 missile.

Skv 336 at Rygge will not re-equip with Fighting Falcons. Its F-5A/B aircraft have been reworked to fit new avionics and extend their service lfe. They should remain operational in the training and ECM roles until the mid-1990s. Two additional Block 15 OCU aircraft were delivered in 1989, but a planned order for eight more aircraft intended to serve as attrition replacements has been shelved.

Non-NATO customers

Given the capability of the F-16, further orders for the aircraft were inevitable. On May 7, 1975, both YF-16s were flown to Cecil Field, Jacksonville, Florida, to carry out flight demonstrations for the Shah of Iran and King Hussein of Jordan. The programme watched by the monarchs included a mock dogfight between the GD aircraft and an F-4 Phantom.

Left: Deployment of the F-16 no doubt strained the logistic facilities of the Egyptian Air Force, but will dramatically improve Egypt's technological capability.

ing Falcons using the longer-range APG-63 radar and AIM-7 Sparrow missiles.

Exact details of the raid have never been published: Israeli accounts contain minimal information, often verging on hagiography rather than combat reporting. The eight aircraft, plus their escort of six F-15s, probably took off from Etzion air base, near Eilat in southern Israel. External tanks were carried and the formation may have begun by topping up from tanker aircraft.

Complete surprise

Tactical surprise was complete, the raiders approaching from the west and reporting some anti-aircraft fire, but no interceptors or SAM launches. The Fighting Falcons attacked in two waves, each consisting of two pairs of aircraft. Prime target was the 105ft (32m) diameter concrete cupola covering the reactor. Individual bomb runs took less than two minutes, the first wave scoring at least two hits with 2,000lb (907kg) Mk 84 bombs.

The reactor was badly damaged, the protective dome collapsing and burying the complex in rubble, while laboratories and other facilities were also damaged and one French technician was killed. The second wave is reported not to have bombed. The attackers were not engaged during the return flight, which took them westwards, back across Jordan and into Israeli airspace. The Reagan administration told Congress that the raid may have been a 'substantial violation' of US/Israeli mutual defense agreements, and placed a temporary embargo on F-16 deliveries to the IDFAF.

Delivery of further F-16s was temporarily embargoed once again on July 17,

Iran became the first third-party nation to adopt the F-16. A letter of intent signed by the Imperial Iranian Government on October 27, 1976, covered the procurement of 160 aircraft, and a follow-on buy of a further 140 was also discussed.

Following the Iranian revolution early in 1979, the new Iranian Government cancelled all the massive arms contracts signed by the former Shah, including the F-16 deal. Work on these aircraft had already started, but only minor components had been built. Discussing the cancellation with the author at the time of the announcement, a GD spokesman pointed out that hardware already built could be switched to other customers, and that the likely beneficiary was Israel.

In terms of cost, the loss of the Iranian order had a more marked effect. The likely cost increase for the USAF was estimated at $175,000 per aircraft, while the price rise of European-built examples was predicted to be $129,000 or more per aircraft.

Israel was virtually a captive market for the F-16. After the 1967 arms embargo on the Mirage 5 fleet, Israel was unlikely to place a major order for warplanes with France, and given the importance of the Arab world as a market, it is unlikely that Dassault-Breguet would want the undesirable publicity of another Israeli aircraft deal.

Price information was originally sought on a package of 250 aircraft, and the Tsvah Haganah le Israel – Heyl ha'Avir (Israel Defence Force – Air Force) was reported to have a long-term requirement for a further 150 to 200 examples. In August 1978 Israel announced plans to procure 75 aircraft under a contract valued at around $1·2 billion. This purchase was split between 67 F-16As and eight F-16Bs, and was expected to lead in the longer term to a total purchase of 225 aircraft by the end of the 1980s.

A total of 17 modifications to the Fighting Falcon were requested by the IDFAF: Israeli aircraft would carry weapons not used by other F-16 operators, while IDFAF training and mission-management techniques differed from USAF/NATO practice. Hardware and software had to be modified to meet these specific national requirements.

Deliveries to Israel started on July 2, 1980, at a rate of four per month under a schedule which should have seen the last handed over in November 1981. Flown by US personnel drawn from the 16th Tactical Training Squadron, the first four made the journey from Florida to Israel in 11 hours. An excellent demonstratioin of the type's long range, this sortie required the use of full external tanks and three in-flight refuellings.

The Osirak raid

Less than 14 months after entering IDFAF service, the Fighting Falcon went to war. On June 7, 1981, eight were used in a precision air strike against the Osirak nuclear reactor being built at Twartha near Baghdad. Due to become operational in the late summer or early autumn of 1981, this facility was seen as a threat to Israeli security. According to Israeli intelligence, if allowed to 'go critical', the 70MW Osirak reactor would have turned out sufficient plutonium to allow Iraq to construct up to five 20kT nuclear weapons by the mid-1980s.

Timing of the raid was critical. The longer it was delayed, the more complete Osirak would be at the moment of its destruction, and thus the greater the losses in equipment suffered by Iraq. At the same time, it was essential that the raid be conducted before the reactor began operating, lest its destruction released a cloud of intensely radioactive material into the atmosphere.

Selection of the F-16 for the Osirak mission resulted from several factors, including the type's long range, the ground-mapping modes available on the APG-66 radar, and the accuracy of the navigation and attack systems. Eight aircraft formed the strike component of the mission, while six F-15 Eagles flew top cover in order to protect the Fight-

Below: One result of the Soviet invasion of Afghanistan was clearance for Pakistan to receive US warplanes – F-16s rather than the A-7 Corsair IIs originally requested.

Right: As US/Israeli relations grew more strained following the Osirak raid and 1982 invasion of Lebanon, the supply of further F-16s to the IDFAF was repeatedly embargoed.

1981, following a week-long series of attacks on Palestinian bases in the Lebanon. At this point 53 aircraft had been delivered, and ten more were due to begin their flight to Israel that day. Delivery of all 75 aircraft to Israel was eventually completed by the end of 1981. In May 1982 the US Congress was told that the Reagan Administration intended to supply a further 75 F-16Cs and Ds to the IDFAF, with deliveries starting in 1985.

The spring and summer of 1982 saw IDFAF Fighting Falcons in action once again. In the course of air combat over the Bekaa valley in Lebanon the Israeli Air Force claimed the destruction of 92 Syrian fighters, more than half of which were MiG-23 Floggers. In this air-to-air fighting the F-16 emerged as the top-scoring 'MiG-killer', downing 44 Syrian warplanes, while the F-15 accounted for a further 40. Most of the kills were scored using the AIM-9L 'all-aspect' version of Sidewinder.

Aircraft most commonly met in combat by the Israeli pilots were the MiG-21, MiG-23 and Su-22. Syrian tactics were poor, according to the Israeli pilots, with little evidence of careful pre-flight planning. There was no shortage of bravery, however – wave upon wave of Syrian aircraft rushed into combat despite their heavy losses.

Peace Mobile II

Not until 1986 that the first F-16C and -D aircraft for the IDFAF left the production line. All 75 had been delivered by the end of 1988 under the Peace Marble II programme.

Israel had asked that these F-16C and D be fitted with the latest IPE version of the F110 turbofan, but this was refused. Israel's Bet Shemesh Engines embarked on its own F110 uprating programme. The resulting F110-GE-110A engine sacrifices engine lifetime in exchange for a thrust boost of up to 50 per cent at low level. The uprated engine was under test by the summer of 1990.

First aircraft to receive the new engine were 24 F-16Ds which had been locally converted into specialised two-seat fighters for missions such as "Wild Weasel"-style anti-radar strikes. These aircraft can be recognised by the presence of a massive dorsal spine. Similar to that on the MiG-21bis, it provides the additional avionics space needed.

The first prototype of the indigenous Israel Aircraft Industries Lavi fighter began flight trials on 31st December 1986. By the time that two had been flown, rising costs and a reluctance by the US to continue bankrolling the programme forced cancellation in early 1988. Long-term plans had to be drawn up around the F-16.

Peace Marble III announced in August 1988 covers the supply of 60 more Fighting Falcons. Based on the F-16D and incorporating some Israeli avionics, these are expected to enter service from 1990/91 onwards. The final examples are due to leave the line late in 1992. Known changes to the aircraft include a customised radar, improved central air-data computer, and better EW systems.

A requirement exists for 75 more aircraft. This proposed Peace Marble IV programme would involve Block 50 aircraft upgraded with Israeli-requested changes in areas such as radar and EW.

These Peace Vector I aircraft were Block 15 models, so lacked MSIP avionics, but were modified to meet specific Egyptian requirements. For example, they are fitted with the same

Above: Due in service in 1991 and 1992, this is an artist's impression of the Israeli F-16D, featuring new Israeli-developed avionices.

Teledyne IFF system as all other EAF fighters, including modernised Soviet types.

Problems experienced in operating a batch of ex-USAF F-4 Phantoms delivered in 1979 had made Egypt aware of the technological gulf between Soviet and US warplanes. This time, the EAF was determined to make sure it had the infrastructure needed to support the new fighter.

Ground crew attended training courses in the USA before the aircraft were delivered, so that maintenance facilities would be prepared and personnel trained by the time the first Fighting Falcons arrived. General Dynamics built maintenance hangers and an underground avionics repair shop at An Shas air base, 30 miles (50km) northeast of Cairo, and 114 US technicians were sent to Egypt to help service the GD aircraft.

Aircraft for the Egyptian Air Force started down the line in 1981. The first was handed over at Fort Worth on January 15, 1982, and the first batch arrived at An Shas air base on March 24. The 41st aircraft left the production line at the end of 1983.

A follow-on Peace Vector II programme was already under way by this time. As part of a $1,300 million package of military sales credits for Egypt requested from Congress in 1982, an agreement covering the supply of 40 F-16 C and D aircraft was signed in May 1982. These aircraft were built in 1986/7.

Peace Vector III covers a further 40 C and D models ordered in November 1987, plus a single D ordered in 1989 to replace a lost F-16A. These aircraft will be built in 1991/2 on a schedule a few months ahead of Israel's Peace Marble III batch. These aircraft will be armed with the AIM-7 Sparrow, which will be

launched using the high pulse-rate track mode of the aircraft's APG-66(V) radar.

In 1989 the US Government agreed to supply Egypt with twelve sets of Martin-Marietta Pathfinder navigation pods and Sharpshooter targeting pods. Derivatives of LANTIRN, these will enter service on EAF F-16s in 1991.

Egypt wants more F-16s. In August 1990 the US offered a further 40, but Egypt announced its intention to obtain 40 from the Turkish production line at Murted. The new aircraft will probably enter service in the mid-1990s.

On June 25, 1980, Egypt signed a letter of agreement covering the supply of 40 F-16s. The deal was worth more than $960 million and included the 40 aircraft, ten spare F100 engines, and ordnance including 600 Maverick

Below: Painted with temporary US markings and loaded with external tanks, a Fighting Falcon begins the long trans-Atlantic/trans-Mediterranean trip which will end some 11 hours later in delivery to the Israeli Defence Force – Air Force.

rounds, 500lb (227kg) and 1,000lb (454kg) bombs and 20mm cannon ammunition. Also included were a simulator plus other support equipment and manuals.

Egypt originally wanted the F-15, and despite having the F-16 on order still wanted the Eagle, presumably as part of a 'Hi-Lo' mix. By 1980 it was obvious that the McDonnell Douglas warplane was too expensive for Egypt's limited budget and the likely level of US military credit available, so this plan was abandoned, at least for the time being.

Diversions to Egypt

Growing unserviceability of Soviet-supplied warplanes made early delivery of the Fighting Falcon essential, and in order to meet Egyptian requests that deliveries be speeded up 30 examples were diverted from the USAF. Between December 1981 and May 1983 monthly deliveries to the USAF were cut from 15 aircraft to around 13. The remaining ten EAF F-16s were built from scratch as export aircraft.

Egypt has a total requirement for 120 F-16s to replace part of the aging fleet of Soviet-supplied MiGs and Sukhois. Given the high cost of Western defence equipment compared to Soviet products, the EAF was unable to replace Fishbeds and Fitters on a one-for-one basis, so the nominal size of the service declined during the 1980s.

F-16s for Korea

President Carter's idealistic plan, announced in 1977, to withdraw 39,000 US troops from South Korea was soon to be suspended as the 1970s drew to a close, but triggered off that nation's equipment upgrading plans. A requirement for 100 new fighters was identified, and US approval for the purchase of 72 aircraft was requested in 1979.

South Korea took delivery of the first of a batch of 30 F-16C and 6 F-16D in early 1986. By the time that the last examples had arrived in early 1989, South Korea was planning to buy more fighters. Following evaluations of the F-16 and F-18, in December 1989 it became the first export nation to opt for a mix of F-16s and F-18s, ordering 120 of the latter aircraft.

In the spring of 1991 South Korea cancelled its F-18 order, saying that the aircraft cost had risen to an unacceptable degree. This was largely due to the high rate of inflation in the USA. Under a deal agreed in the summer of 1991, South Korea is to build a further batch of F-16s under licence. These will be to the Block 50 standard, and powered by the P&W F100-PW-229 engine.

The first 12 aircraft would be built by GD, a further 36 supplied at knocked-down kits, and the remaining 72 built under licence by Samsung Aerospace Industries. South Korea was another early LANTIRN user, placing an order for ten systems in 1990.

Following the Soviet intervention in Afghanistan in December 1979, the US agreed to supply F-16s to Pakistan, which became the ninth nation to adopt the type. Contracts covering the supply of 40 Block 15 aircraft were signed in December 1981.

Deliveries were delayed when Pakistan refused to accept the ALR-46(V)-3 radar-warning receiver fitted to the aircraft, and insisted on being supplied with the more advanced ALR-69. Clearance for the latter system was finally granted, allowing handover of the first aircraft in October 1982. A second batch of 11 aircraft ordered in 1988 is now in service, and third batch of 60 are due to start arriving in 1992. Some of the current fleet have been fitted with Thomson-CSF Atlis II laser designator/ranger pods.

In 1983 Turkey ordered 128 F110-

powered F-16C and 32 F-16D for service with the Turk Hava Kuvvetleri (Turkish Air Force). The first aircraft was handed over in July 1987, and was followed by seven more GD-built examples.

The remainder are being built in Turkey by the TUSAS consortium. Deliveries from the Murted production line started in 1988, and all of this first batch should be completed by 1995. The first 44 aircraft built at Murted were Block 30, and entered service with the 141 Filo, then the 142 Filo. The remaining 101 F016C and 15 F015D will be Block 40.

In 1990 Turkey opened negotiations with the USA for a follow-on production run. This is likely to number around 200. 160 would be for the Turkish Air Force; 40 for Egypt.

Turkey was one of the first export customers for the LANTIRN system, placing an order for 40 systems in late 1990.

During the early 1980s, Greece's choice of a new aircraft to re-equip the Elliniki Aeroporia was subject to repeated postponements, but that country finally announced that its requirement for less than 100 aircraft would be split between the US and France. The orders were for 34 F-16C and 6 F-16D, plus 40 Mirage 2000. First into service was the Mirage, with deliveries of 2000E (single-seat) and B (two-seat) fighters beginning in March 1988. Eight months later, the first Fighting Falcons arrived. By the end of 1989, all the F-16s had been delivered. Another squadron is to be re-equipped for the anti-shipping role. This will involve a follow-on order for 20 F-16s or Mirages.

Greece will eventually need to replace older aircraft such as the F-5 and F-104, but for the moment fleet levels are being maintained by the acquisition of ex-Klu F-5s and ex-Luftwaffe F-104s.

For many years, Portugal has had no

modern fighter, having to rely on elderly types such as the F-8 Crusader and G.91. US military credits offered in 1989 covered a batch of 20 ex-USAF F-16A/B fighters.

The F-16 has proved an effective replacement for the Northrop F-5E and F. Bahrain has been an F-5 operator since 1986, and was offered the F-16 in the following year. A batch of 12 F110-powered F-16C/D was delivered in 1990. A follow-on order for four more aircraft was placed in mid-1988. Bahrain was also the first export customer to arm its Fighting Falcons with the AIM-7 Sparrow.

Like Bahrain, Indonesia had kept its F-5s in service, supplementing them with 12 Fighting Falcons. The first of 12 Block 15 OCU F-16A/B powered by the uprated F100-PW-220 engine was not handed over at Fort Worth until October 1989, and the type became operational in 1990.

Asian nations also joined the growing numbers of F-16 operators. Worried that its fleet of F-5E/F and earlier A/B models was outclassed by Vietnam's new MiG-23 Floggers, Thailand ordered a batch of 12 F-16 Block 15 OCU in 1985. These entered service in 1988, by which time a follow-on batch of six had been ordered for delivery in 1991.

Singapore was due to be the first F-5 operator to field the downgraded J79-powered version of the Fighting Falcon, placing an order for eight in 1984. When Thailand was cleared in 1985 to order the standard F-16A/B, Singapore insisted on being allowed to switch its order for eight aircraft to the Block 15 OCU F-16A/B model. This effectively killed off the F-16/79 programme. The Block 15 aircraft were built in 1988, and entered service in 1990 following crew training in the USA.

The sole Latin-American F-16 user is Venezuela, which in 1982 ordered 16

Block 15 F-16A and eight F-16B. Delivered between 1983 and 1985, these supplemented an existing fleet of Mirage IIIE.

In 1987, Japan announced that its next fighter – the FS-X (Fighter, Support, experimental), would be a derivative of either the F-16 or the F-15. Intended as a replacement for the Mitsubishi F-1, the chosen airframe would be fitted with selected items of Japanese technology such as a phased-array radar and a new fire-control system, and would also incorporate Japanese-developed stealth technology.

The final choice announced in October of that year was the SX-3, a big-wing F-16 derivative fitted with canards, and using advanced technology composite materials in the forward and aft fuselage sections, and in the increased-span wings. The prime contractor would be Mitsubishi.

Although recognisably an F-16 derivative, the SX-3 has a stretched aft fuselage, longer-span co-cured composite wings, twin manoeuvring canards beneath the inlet, a reprofiled nose, a strengthened canopy, and a drag chute. This extensive re-design which will leave only some 20 to 30 per cent of the airframe unchanged.

Japanese-developed RAM materials will be used to reduce radar signature, and the entire leading edge of the long-span composite wings will incorporate RAM, presumably to reduce front-sector RCS.

Mitsubishi Electric was given the job of developing a high-resolution active phased-array radar able to switch rapidly between air-to-air and air-to-ground modes. Under a $67 million contract, the company completed four engineering models, one of which started flight trials in 1991 aboard a Kawasaki C-1 transport.

SX-3 will have an enhanced-manoeuvrability flight-control system able to extract the best performance from its ventral canard surfaces. This will offer fully-decoupled flight modes, including

the ability to fly with its nose angled to the line of flight.

The US Government refused to give Mitsubishi access to the source code of the latest F-16 flight-control software, so Japan decided to develop its own. Once this problem had been solved, full-scale development was able to begin in the summer of 1991.

After evaluating the latest versions of the P&W F100 and GE F110, Japan decided in 1991 to adopt the GE engine. The chosen powerplant will be an uprated version of the F110-GE-129, developing around 31,000lb (14,000kg) of thrust. GE is to supply four engines in the mid-1990s for use in the prototypes. Production of around 150 engines will begin in the late 1990s, and will probably be tackled by Ishikawajima-Harima.

Armament will include several types of Japanese-developed missile, including the Mitsubishi Type 80 ASM-1 anti-ship missile, and the new Mitsubishi AAM-3 agile air-to-air weapon currently being developed to replace the AIM-9L

Above: An artist's impression of the Japanese SX-3. Derived from the F-16 by Mitsubishi Electric, full-scale development began in 1991.

Sidewinder on aircraft such as the F-15J, and F-4J. This missile completed 13 months of operational testing in 1989/90. According to the JASDF, the AAM-3 IR seeker is better than those of all contemporary weapons.

Under the original schedule, the SX-3 would have flown in 1993, with production deliveries beginning in 1997. A total of 130 would be built by the year 2001 at a predicted unit cost of $35. By the end of 1990, it was obvious that this was over-optimistic. Changes to the design and the need to develop flight-control software added delays and increased the cost.

SX-3 will not fly until the mid-1990s, entering service in 1999. Projected costs will be at least 40 per cent above original estimates. The number to be bought will be between 100 and 130.

Performance and Handling

Ready for takeoff on an air-combat mission with no external tanks, Fighting Falcon tips the scales at around half the weight of an F-4 or F-15 tasked with a similar mission. Even by the standards of classic lightweight designs such as the MiG-21 Fishbed and Dassault-Breguet Mirage III, the F-16 is still a light fighter, weighing about one third more than the Soviet fighter and twelve per cent more than the Dassault delta. The GD aircraft matches its light weight with combat performance which the Mirage or MiG pilot can only dream about and a weapon delivery accuracy better than that of the F-111.

A lightly loaded F-16 with full internal fuel has a thrust-to-weight ratio of just over 1:1 in full afterburner. Working with the lightweight YF-16 prototypes, GD test pilots carried out pre-takeoff engine and system checks at 80 per cent power. Application of full afterburning power would have caused the wheels to slide.

Fighting Falcon begins its take-off roll with the wing leading and trailing-edge flaps positioned 2deg up and 20deg down respectively. After brake release, the aircraft quickly picks up speed. Rotation is usually at around 125kt, liftoff at around 140kt.

When Robert Ropelewski of *Aviation Week* flew the F-16B for the first time in 1979, GD Chief test pilot Neil Anderson was able to demonstrate the takeoff performance: "Anderson ... rotated the nose upwards, stopping at 60deg pitch as the aircraft began climbing out". Given the 30deg reclining tilt of the Fighting Falcon ejection seat, this climb angle meant that the torsos of the two pilots were literally horizontal. The F-16 can climb vertically, but this would result in the pilot hanging head-down in his seat.

"Acceleration continued, even in that attitude", reported Ropelewski, "the aircraft passing through 170kt about 30 seconds after brake release. A wing-over manoeuvre was used to level the aircraft at around 8,000ft (2,450m) altitude, still within the length of the Carswell (AFB) runway. A USAF Northrop T-38 chase aircraft which had started its takeoff roll on the same runway five seconds after the F-16 was just lifting off the runway below."

When the undercarriage is retracted the leading edge changes to 20deg down, while the gain of the flight-control system is doubled to reach its normal flight value. (The 50 per cent reduction while on the ground was incorporated as a result of the inadvertent first flight of the original YF-16 prototype). Throughout the mission the flight-control system remains at full gain, except when the door which covers the refuelling receptacle is opened. The latter operation reduce the control response in pitch and roll by an amount designed to make the aircraft 'less nervous', during the approach to the tanker, refuelling and subsequent separation.

One of the most novel features of the F-16 cockpit is the sidestick controller used in place of the traditional control column. This is located on the starboard side of the cockpit, and incorporates an adjustable armrest mounted on the cockpit wall. This is essential in high-g flight conditions, and includes an optional wrist rest which may be folded back against the wall if not required.

The original pattern of sidestick controller did not move, but was force sensitive only. Although effective, this scheme provided no indication to the pilot of when maximum input was being demanded. To avoid sprained wrists in the excitement of high-g manoeuvres, the USAF decided to allow the definitive design of stick a few millimetres of movement to provide the required degree of 'feedback' to the pilot. The rudder pedals have around 0.5in (1cm) of movement.

The flight-control system ensures that the pilot cannot over-stress the airframe. No matter how hard he operates the controls, the angle of attack and load factor are limited, ensuring that he cannot demand more than 25deg angle of attack or 9g load factor.

In practice, the 9g figure is probably close to the limit that the human body can take while performing a useful military mission. In conventional cockpits, pilots often experience tunnel vision – commonly known as grey-out – at levels of around 6 or 7g, but the semi-reclining seat of the F-16 seems to extend this limit by up to 2g. *Aviation Week's* Robert Ropelewski noted no vision problems at manoeuvres of 8g or more, despite having had grey-out at around 7g in other aircraft.

Above: Even in dry thrust the F-16 is capable of impressive aerobatics. In combat, the added impetus of the afterburner offers the pilot 'brute force' solutions to any desired manoeuvre, while his opponent might have to conserve energy.

Right: The superb visibility of the F-16's canopy is illustrated by this view of aircraft from the 8th TFW. If the pilot looked round he would be able to see his own vertical stabilizer.

The brisk acceleration of the F-16 is a feature which has attracted much comment from pilots. Neil Anderson quotes one of the USAF pilots who tested the YF-16 as saying that flying the F-16 was '... like riding on top of a telegraph pole. Every time you light the afterburner, you are a little nervous that it is going to run out from under you'.

Any feeling that the pilot rides on top of the Fighting Falcon rather than within it is heightened by a bulbous canopy large enough to allow the pilot to look over his shoulder and observe his vertical stabilizer and see whether or not he is leaving a con-trial. Pilots used to the more traditional pattern of low-drag canopy used on such aircraft as the F-4 or A-7 are likely to feel somewhat exposed. At relatively modest bank

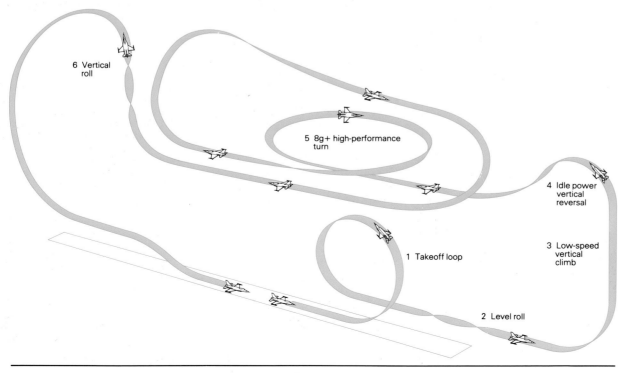

6 Vertical roll

5 8g+ high-performance turn

4 Idle power vertical reversal

1 Takeoff loop

3 Low-speed vertical climb

2 Level roll

Above: Neil Anderson (left), Chief Test Pilot at General Dynamics, played a major role in the F-16 programme. Colleague James McKinney (right) flew the aircraft during the 1979 and 1981 Paris Air Shows.

Left: This composite diagram illustrates some of the manoeuvres flown by the F-16 at Farnborough and Paris Air Shows during the late 1970s.

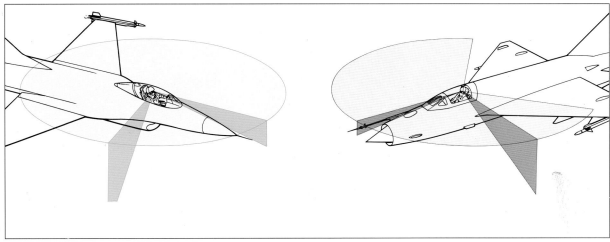

angles the pilot is able to look vertically downward at the terrain below, while the absence of canopy frames in the forward field of view removes the reference points by which pilots instinctively position the horizon during normal flight. During initial Fighting Falcon sorties, new pilots are recommended to fly by instruments until they become accustomed to the external view.

In high-speed cruise the wing leading and trailing-edge flaps are positioned 2deg above centre. Should the pilot attempt maximum-rate manoeuvres, the leading edge will move to 25deg down and the trailing edge will move to neutral. Vortexes generated by the leading-edge strakes play a significant part in improving the handling of the Fighting Falcon, producing improved

Above: Visibility from the cockpit of the F-16 is greatly superior to that from the MiG-21bis.

Left: F-16B two-seater flies an impressive-looking 9g climbing turn.

airflow over the wings and vertical tail. Lift, pitch and directional stability are all improved, while buffet intensity is reduced. Hard manoeuvring at high supersonic speeds can result in some buffeting, according to GD, but for most of the performance envelope Fighting Falcon is buffet-free. Transition through the transonic region is smooth, with only a slight buffeting as speed is increased through Mach 0.95.

Direct comparison between different fighters is always difficult, and the results of any fly-offs are usually classified. GD's own computer modelling of aircraft with a 50 per cent fuel load and two IR missiles and flying in full afterburner makes interesting reading.

At a 1g sustained load factor the F-16 at worst near-matches, and in most cases surpasses its rivals at most combinations of altitude and Mach number. Only at the top right portion of the envelope – between Mach 1.7 at 20,000ft (6,100m) and

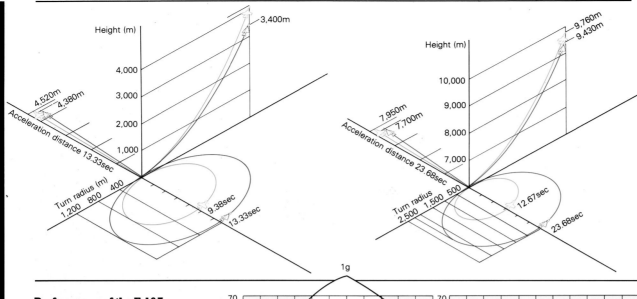

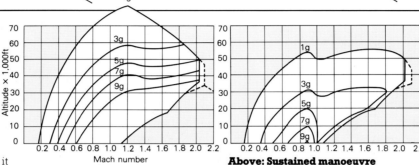

Performance of the F-16A compared with that of the MiG-21bis third-generation version of the Fishbed fighter. The diagrams assume a speed of Mach 0.85 at sea level (above) and 20,000ft (6,000m) (right). In all cases turning performance, acceleration and rate of climb are superior to those of the MiG.

Above: This chart shows the instananeous manoeuvre capability of the turbojet-powered F-16/79. Export clients were unimpressed.

Above: Sustained manoeuvre capability of the F-16/79 is lower than the instantaneous capability, but the ability to sustain 7g is available in the most likely combat conditions.

Mach 1.6 at 55,000ft (16,750m) – is it eclipsed by the Mirage 2000C, an aircraft whose engine was optimised for flight at high supersonic speed.

At a 5g sustained loading, the F-16 dominates the right-hand side of the envelope, with the Rafale A showing better altitude capability between Mach 0.6 and 1.1.

On an air-to-air mission with two IR missiles and two radar missiles, an F-16 maximum external fuel has a tactical radius of 780nm (1,444km) when flying a typical intercept mission. Equivalent figure for the MiG-29 is only 310nm (5674km).

International air shows in the late 1980s saw the F-16 flying show routines alongside its main rivals – the F-18, Mirage 2000 and MiG-29. This allowed GD to publish some unclassified relative performance figures. Most showed the F-16 as superior to its rivals including the EAP and Rafale A. For example, time taken to establish a suitable bank angle, turn 360 degrees at level altitude, then roll out was only 16.3 seconds for the F-16 compared with 16.6 secs (Rafale A), 17.5 secs (MiG-29), 17.8 secs (F/A-18A), 19 secs (EAP) and 24 secs (Mirage 2000C).

According to the RNethAF, the F-16 is "unbeatable" in simulated air combat. By early 1981 the aircraft had been flown against USAFE F-15 Eagles from Bitburg and Soesterberg in West Germany, and against RNethAF Mirage 5B fighters. The radar gave the service a level of look-down performance totally lacking in earlier types such as the F-104G.

Fighting Falcon is also an effective strike aircraft. Even at high speed and low altitude, air turbulence does create significant aircraft instability. Ropelewski has reported flying at 600kts at 100ft (30m) altitude with impressive results. "The aircraft was flyable hands-off, with no indication of gust upsets or even the slightest vertical or lateral accelerations."

During bombing practice, F-16 crews have displayed accuracies well above

Right: Con-trails forming from the strakes of this F-16 trace the path of the vortexes passing over the wing. These streams of energized air greatly enhance flying qualities.

Above: Despite its relatively large wing area, the Fighting Falcon offers pilots a smooth ride at low altitudes and high air speeds, essential qualities for the strike role.

those obtained with earlier tactical fighters. According to the USAF, 2,000lb (907kg) iron bombs can be dropped within 30ft (9m) of a target, compared with the 150ft (45m) typical using the F-4. The best crews of the Korean-based 8th TFW were scoring CEPs (circular error probable) of 9ft (2.74m) during 10deg diving attacks, while the average figure for the unit was 35ft (11m). Given this sort of accuracy, some pilots argue, there is no need to carry guided missiles or 'smart' bombs unless small hard targets such as bridges are to be attacked.

In substituting the GE J79 turbojet in place of the F100 to create the F-16/79 FX export fighter, GD has paid some performance penalty. Two years after his F-16B sortie, Ropelewski was able to fly the F-16/79 and noted a lower takeoff performance. "Acceleration is slower than with the F100 engine and the initial climb attitude is less impressive – in the neighbourhood of 30deg pitch compared with around 60deg for the standard aircraft – in a typical air-to-air configuration."

As the undercarriage is lowered prior to landing, the wing leading and trailing-edge flaps return to the 15 & 20deg down high-lift configuration used for the initial climb, while control sensitivity is reduced by 50 per cent to eliminate any possibility of over-correction.

Typical approach speed is around 125kt, with the aircraft touching down at or just below 120kt. After landing the nose is held up at an angle of 13deg to

Right: In seeking a replacement for the ageing Northrop T-38 Talon, the USAF's Thunderbirds display team finally adopted the Fighting Falcon. It was first used during the 1983 season.

obtain aerodynamic braking, the nose-wheel not being lowered until speed has dropped to around 100kt. Typical landing runs at an aircraft weight of 20,000lb (9,000kg) are around 3,000ft (900m) on dry asphalt or concrete.

The problem of dead-stick landing is of concern to the pilot of any 'hot' single-engined aircraft. To make sure that the Fighting Falcon driver would have confidence in his aircraft should the engine fail, a series of dead-stick landing trials were carried out using the YF-16. Initial tests showed that the aircraft could glide at around 150kt with undercarriage and flaps down, but a figure of 170kt was later chosen.

Below: Without its electronic fly-by-wire system the F-16 would not be controllable.

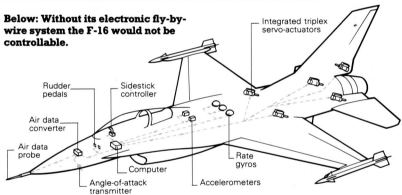

Experimental and Future Variants

Above: The FloTrak wrap-around may look clumsy if not downright agricultural, but trials have shown that with its aid an F-16 could be towed across waterlogged ground, or taxied over a rough field.

Like most successful designs, the F-16 has the potential for development into more advanced versions. Few aircraft can have been subjected to quite so many re-engining and rebuild programmes at such an early stage of their career: within ten years of the first flight by a prototype experimental versions have included an aircraft able to taxi on rain-drenched soil, experimental delta-winged variants, CCV configurations pioneering new ways to fly, forward-swept wings and even a proposed vectored-thrust STOVL model. One thing is certain – the story is unlikely to stop with the aircraft described here.

Fighting Falcon has been used as a testbed for several experimental programmes. In some cases the aircraft was simply a convenient guinea-pig, but other projects involved drastic rebuilds and could lead to more advanced future versions of the F-16.

One of the YF-16 prototypes was used in 1982 to test a novel method of operating high-performance aircraft from damaged airfields. The USAF asked Vehicle System Development Corporation of California to devise a method of allowing jet fighters to be taxied over rough or soft ground. This would allow

Below: Fighting Falcon of the future? Equipped with intake-mounted canards and a MiG-21 style dorsal spine, the ATFI/F-16 is engaged in research which could lead to entirely new types of combat manoeuvre.

aircraft trapped in hardened shelters at bases attacked by anti-airfield weapons such as JP233 to be taken from their shelters and taxied to a takeoff site without using the damaged or mined taxiways.

Wrap-around tracks

The solution devised was to fit wrap-around tracks to the nose and main wheels. These effectively widened and lengthened the 'footprint' of each wheel, reducing ground pressure and, consequently, the chance of the aircraft bogging down in soft terrain. Normal ground pressure of an F-16 is around 275lb/sq in (19kg/sq cm), but the use of the FloTrak wrap-arounds reduces this to just under 80lb/sq in (5·5kg/sq cm). During trials held at Wright-Patterson AFB, Ohio, a YF-16 fitted with FloTraks was able to taxi over rough ground at

speeds of up to 35kt, and was towed across rain-soaked soft ground. At one point during the latter test the wheels of the towing tractor began to sink into the waterlogged soil, but the YF-16 was still free to move.

One of the YF-16 prototypes was rebuilt in the mid-1970s as part of the USAF Flight Dynamics Laboratory Control-Configured Vehicle (CCV) programme. Canard surfaces were added beneath the air intake, one on each side of the nose wheel, the fuel system was modified to allow greater control over the position of the aircraft centre of gravity, and the flight-control system was modified to allow the aircraft to be manoeuvred in ways not possible with conventional controls.

In a normal aircraft, movements in one plane are often related to movements in another. For example, in order

to turn, a conventional aircraft must bank. On the YF-16/CCV, movements are fully independent or 'decoupled'. The aircraft can rise or fall using direct lift, move laterally by direct side force, or yaw, pitch or roll independently of direction of flight.

GD test pilot David J. Thigpen flew the modified aircraft in its new configuration for the first time on March 16, 1976, starting what was scheduled to be a programme of 85 flights. While coming in to land at the end of the 29th CCV test mission on June 24, 1976, the aircraft suffered a loss of engine power while still some half a mile from touchdown. Thigpen brought the aircraft down in a rough landing, but the undercarriage collapsed under the strain. Subsequent repairs took more than six months, flights resuming in the spring of 1977.

The flight-test programme was completed by the end of July of that year. After 125 hours of experimental flying (87 flights), the YF-16/CCV proved that the new degrees of freedom such as fuselage pointing measurably improved mission effectiveness, and that future aircraft incorporating CCV technology could be designed to be smaller, lighter, less expensive and more manoeuvrable than conventional types.

The AFTI/F-16

Advances in electronic technology resulting from digital systems and large-scale integrated circuits suggest that future fighters will be able to incorporate new types of flight-control and nav/attack systems. To evaluate these, the USAF has devised the Advanced Fighter Technology Integration (AFTI) programme. This uses a heavily modified F-16 as a testbed, GD having been awarded a contract on December 26, 1978, to rebuild one of the full-scale development F-16s. The aircraft was handed over to the company in March 1980.

The AFTI/F-16 is immediately recognizable by the presence of intake-mounted canard surfaces and a dorsal spine similar to that fitted to third-generation MiG-21s. The latter modification provides the internal volume needed to house flight-test equipment. The AFTI/F-16 has a triplex digital flight-control system which will give the pilot CCV-type freedom of manoeuvre. All movements are fully decoupled.

First flight of the modified aircraft was delayed by software problems, but finally took place at Fort Worth on July 10, 1982. The first three test flights were carried out at Fort Worth by GD pilots, and the aircraft was then flown to Edwards AFB, California, to begin a two-year programme of 275 test flights.

The first year of flying explored the unorthodox flight modes such as fuselage pointing and direct-force translation. Early sorties checked aircraft behaviour over a large portion of the performance envelope, before work began on proving the digital flight control system and the new degrees of freedom which it permits.

Pilots explored the effects of adding decoupled degrees of freedom to normal flight, determining how the new freedom of manoeuvre can best be used, and how unconventional motions and attitudes affect the pilot. It had been anticipated that some manoeuvres might cause vertigo or nausea in pilots, making them of little use in combat.

At the end of this phase, the aircraft

Below: First F-16 to explore the strange world of decoupled flight movements was the YF-16/CCV. A series of 87 flights by the rebuilt prototype the mid-1970s paved the way for the more recent AFTI/F-16.

was returned to Fort Worth for further updating, so that integrated flight and fire-control tests could begin.

This involved installing an Automatic Manoeuvring Attack System (AMAS), whose main components were a Westinghouse sensor pod containing a FLIR sensor and laser rangefinder, a helmet-mounted sight, digital fire-control computer, radar altimeter and a Standard Avionics-Integrated Fuzing (SAIF) unit.

The sensor pod was mounted in the port wing root, sharing the digital programmable signal processor of the APG-66 radar. In operational use, the pod could be slaved to the radar, helmet sight, or inertial navigation system so that targets detected by the latter could be tracked by passive infra-red means. On an operational fighter, this would reduce the amount of time during which the aircraft must transmit. The pod could also be used to acquire targets independently.

Data from the FLIR was passed to the integrated flight/fire-control system, which generated the steering commands needed to steer the aircraft automatically towards the target.

Following these trials – which won the 1987 Theodore von Karman Award for outstanding contribution to science and engineering – the F-16/AFTI found itself

in regular use as a testbed for new technologies. For a series of CAS/BAI (Close Air Support/Battlefield Air Interdiction) trials aimed at proving technology for a possible attack version of the F-16, the canards were removed. This programme was focussed on electro-optical sensors such as a laser spot tracker and an ejection-safe helmet mounted display linked to a head-steered FLIR sensor.

Between early 1988 and the summer of 1991, the aircraft had flown four series of CAS trials, and was starting the first tests of a pilot-activated attitude recovery system. Similar in concept to that carried by the Soviet MiG-29, it can be used in the event of the pilot becoming disoriented. Pressing a switch on the control stick automatically returns the aircraft to level flight with the nose slightly high. This modification had been carried out to increase safety during a planned series of night-time flight tests of integrated helmet night-vision systems.

In 1980, news of a new and drastically modified F-16 variant was leaked to the US technical press. Designated SCAMP (Supersonic Cruise and Manoeuvring Prototype), this was based on studies carried out by GD between 1976 and 1980, and featured a 'cranked' delta wing, a configuration proposed to the USAF by GD in February 1980. Although the programme was at this stage

Above: Seen from this angle the F-16/XL bears a distinct resemblance to Fort Worth's biggest delta – the Convair B-58 Hustler. Note how the stores are mounted close to the underside of the wing.

a private venture by the manufacturer, the USAF did provide support, and the third and sixth full-scale development F-16s were returned to GD in the summer of 1981 for conversion to the new configuration.

Given the large production base of the F-16, GD designers tried to capitalize on existing components and experience in order to reduce the potential cost of the new variant. Wings and horizontal tail account for about 11 per cent of the total cost of the F-16, and these are the main all-new components in what was now designated the F-16XL. Although the rebuild did involve a modest fuselage stretch, the new designation did not, as some humorists suggested, stand for 'Xtra Length'!

Despite the significant external differences between the F-16A and the F-16XL, the airframe of the latter has more than 70 per cent commonality with the standard fighter. If a production version were to be ordered by the USAF, this would probably have MSIP-standard avionics, including the

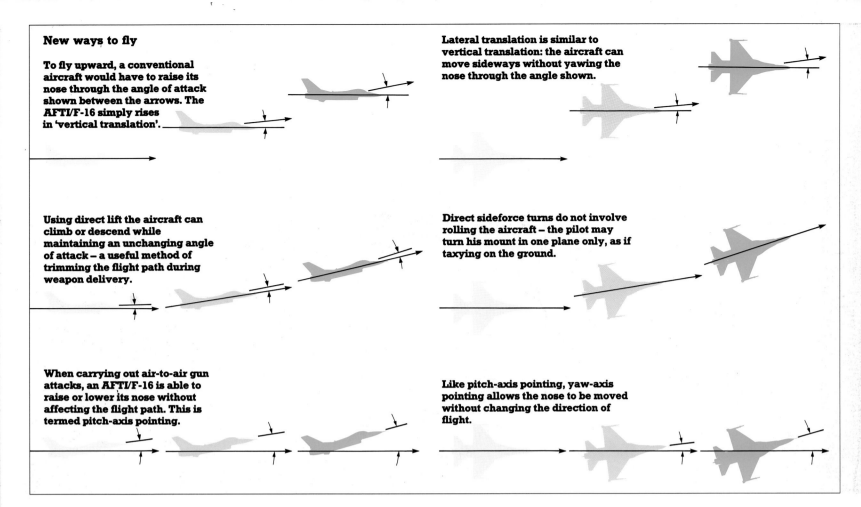

New ways to fly

To fly upward, a conventional aircraft would have to raise its nose through the angle of attack shown between the arrows. The AFTI/F-16 simply rises in 'vertical translation'.

Lateral translation is similar to vertical translation: the aircraft can move sideways without yawing the nose through the angle shown.

Using direct lift the aircraft can climb or descend while maintaining an unchanging angle of attack – a useful method of trimming the flight path during weapon delivery.

Direct sideforce turns do not involve rolling the aircraft – the pilot may turn his mount in one plane only, as if taxying on the ground.

When carrying out air-to-air gun attacks, an AFTI/F-16 is able to raise or lower its nose without affecting the flight path. This is termed pitch-axis pointing.

Like pitch-axis pointing, yaw-axis pointing allows the nose to be moved without changing the direction of flight.

modified radar and LANTIRN.

F-16XL flight tests

First flight of the F-16XL took place at Fort Worth on July 15, 1982. This first sortie was all-subsonic, the aircraft reaching a top speed of Mach 0·9, a height of 30,000ft (9,000m), a maximum load factor of 3g and 20deg of angle of attack. At takeoff the angle of attack was 8deg, rising to 10deg at landing. Both values are well below those associated with traditional delta designs. Test pilot Jim McKinney reported that handling was 'very different' from that of the basic F-16, offering a 'solid ride'.

Following a small number of flights, the aircraft was transferred to Edwards AFB to begin a joint USAF/GD trials programme. Due to run for 240 flights over a period of nine months, this exercise involved both prototypes – the single-seat F100-powered version and the later GE F110-powered two-seater. Tests assessed the 'ride' which the air-

craft offers at low level, and the use of high-speed tactics for defense penetration without the use of afterburner.

The second F-16XL is a two-seat rebuild of a full-scale development F-16A which was damaged in a landing accident. Ground proof-load tests of this aircraft suggested that the aft wing spar would fail at around 85 per cent of the planned limit, so the centre 22in (56cm) section of aluminium spar was replaced by a steel component.

First flight of the second F-16XL took place on October 29, 1982, again from Fort Worth. This aircraft, powered by the GE F110 turbofan, reached Mach 1.4 on its first sortie, with test pilot Alex Wolf in the front cockpit and Jim McKinney in the rear.

During the first 53 hours of F-16XL flight tests a total of seven GD and USAF pilots flew the aircraft. Highlights of this first period of testing included speeds approaching Mach 2·0 and altitudes of up to 50,000ft (15,240m). The aircraft re-

fuelled from a KC-135 tanker, reached a speed of Mach 1·2 while carrying 12 Mk 82 bombs, and ripple-released the same ordnance load during dropping tests. After a brief grounding while further vibration trials were carried out and a braking parachute was installed, the aircraft began a series of stability and control tests, including an exploration of high angles of attack.

The F-16XL was extensively flight tested, and evaluated as a possible next-generation air-to-ground fighter for the USAF. The larger F-15 proved more attractive, and was ordered as the two-seat F-15E.

Late 1991 saw the rollout of another experimental variant. The VISTA/F-16 was designed as a replacement for the USAF's 40 year old NT-33A variable-stability research aircraft. Based on an F-16D, this aircraft added an Israeli-style dorsal spine able to house 948lb (430kg) of variable-stability and data-acquisition electronics. The gun and ammunition

drum were removed to make way for three simulation computers, while the quadruplex FBW system was linked to the new variable-stability system.

When the US Navy drew up specification TS169 for a STOVL (short-take-off/vertical landing) supersonic technology demonstrator, GD proposed the E7. This would have had a modified F-16 fuselage mated with a new delta wing and a GE F110 engine. Vertical lift was to be provided by a "three-poster" configuration, with fan air being ejected downward from nozzles in the wing roots, and an aft-mounted vectoring nozzle. The only hardware to result was a large wind-tunnel model.

Several upgrade schemes have been devised to keep the Fighting Falcon combat effective into the late 1990s. USAF Block 30 aircraft are being upgraded by a programme known as Falcon Push. This updates the avionics software, in some cases adding refinements suggested by service aircrew.

In 1990 Honeywell received a USAF order for an initial batch of 108 H-423 laser INS systems for retrofit to the F-16C and D. Further orders should cover enough hardware to retrofit the entire USAF F-16 fleet.

By the early 1990s the operating costs of a single F-4G Wild Weasel squadron were three times that of an F-16 unit, forcing the USAF to draw up plans to pass these aircraft to the ANG. To replace the F-4G, some F-16s could be equipped to handle the Wild Weasel task.

Possibilities being considered for the F4-G replacement include fitting the aircraft with a datalink able to receive target information from the E-8 JSTARS aircraft, or removing the APR-47 radar homing and warning system from the F-4G and repackaging it in pod-mounted form for use on the F-16. Under a program known as the High Speed Anti-Radiation Missile Targeting System (HTS), the USAF is investigating an

Left: The F-16 that never was – the forward-swept wing demonstrator proposed to DARPA in the mid-1970s.

add-on Wild Weasel pod.

Belgium, Denmark, Netherlands and Norway all plan to upgrade their F-16A/B fleets, a total of around 730 aircraft. Modification kits due to end development by the mid-1990s, will add a modular mission computer able to replace the three current flight-control computers, and improved radar with greater range, track-while-scan capability, and increased reliability, GPS and terrain-reference navaids, and a microwave landing system. An optional helmet-mounted sight is also under study. Total value of the programme is around $2 million.

The Multi-Role Fighter
The Planned replacement for the F-16 is the Multi-Role Fighter (MRF). This programme has a low priority, given that in 1991 the average age of Fighting Falcons assigned to the attack role was only six years. These aircraft will not need replacement until arround 1998 at the earliest.

MRF is unlikely to be an all-new design; the existence of a stealthy F-22 Advanced Tactical Fighter would allow a less stealthy MRF. If this concept is adopted, a developed version of either the F-16 or the F-18 is likely to be selected some time in 1992. Engine and manufacturing development would begin in 1994, allowing production to begin in 1997, followed by an IOC in 2000.

Present plans assume that 2,000 MRF will be bought. MRF could also be sold as an export fighter, replacing many of the F-16s currently in service around the world. One argument in favour of a derivative aircraft is that critical technologies such as stealth could be omitted from some export versions.

GD's concepts of a derivative MRF design were focussed on the Falcon 21. This was virtually a family of designs. The basic configuration used a trapezoidal wing similar to that of the F-22, but with no horizontal stabiliser. This provided a better compromise between the demands of subsonic and supersonic manoeuvrability. Outboard hardpoints

were conventional weapons pylons at mid-span, while four AMRAAM missiles could be carried in conformal mountings against the lower wing/fuselage fairing.

Falcon 21 was a stealthy air-superiority fighter promoted as a possible alternative to the Advanced Tactical Fighter. An evaluation of this design using the TAC Brawler computer model of air-to-air combat showed that this aircraft – like the rival F-15 proposal – could match the ATF in aerodynamic performance but not in terms of low observability. Some ordnance was carried internally, the remainder externally in cocoon mounting. This reduced RCS to below that of the F-15. Development costs of the Falcon 21 would have been around $6 billion – $7 billion, slightly lower than the $7 billion to $8 billion predicted for the F-15, and well below the $12 billion for ATF.

This version probably takes the Fighting Falcon as far as is possible. GD's next design was for an all-new MRF contender. If the money for an all-new design can be found, concept-definition studies could run until late 1995, leading to a four-year demonstration/validation phase, followed by engine and manufacturing development, and a production startup in 2003. Under this programme, IOC would slip by about five years, taking place in 2005.

The design offered by GD is based on an all-composite wing incorporating a system of active aeroelastic wing-section tailoring using new-technology actuation systems. It would combine integrated thrust-vectoring nozzles and new locations for control surfaces.

Thrust-vectoring will not remain the preserve of next-generation fighters such as the F-22 and any all-new MRF. In 1990, P&W and GE revealed that they were experimenting with a new type of thrust-vectoring which relied on a symmetric actuation of the segments which make up the powerplant's variable area nozzle. This could allow the thrust to be vectored in any direction – not just in the

vertical plane as on the F-22 – by angles of up to about 20deg.

Both companies intend to apply the technique to their F-15/F-16 powerplants. Working in conjunction with GD, GE plans to test its vectored-thrust F110 aboard an Israeli Air Force F-16D, probably in 1992. The new nozzles being developed by both companies will be bolt-on fit to existing engines. With retrofits like this taking shape on the drawing board, the F-16 seems assured of a long future.

Above: This head-on view of the F-16/XL illustrates the excellent shape of the basic F-16 canopy. The pilot has good downward visibility on both sides of the fuselage.

Below: Commercially successful world-wide, and now combat proven, the F-16 is to undergo further development to assure its place as a leading combat aircraft.

Glossary and abbreviations

AIM-	US designation for air-to-air missiles	ECP	Engineering Change Proposal	Nr	Number (Dutch)
AFB	Air Force Base	ECP 350	MSIP modification scheme	OCU	Operational Conversion Unit
AGM-	US designation for air-to-surface missiles	Envelope	Engineering term for the area defined by a series of limits	Pacer Loft	Modification programme for European F-16s
AFTI	Advanced Fighter Technology Integration	Esc	see Escadrille and Escuadron	P&W	Pratt & Whitney
Algorithm	Mathematical process for achieving a desired result	Escadrille	Squadron (Belgium)	Raster scan	Method of building up a TV-style image on a CRT by scanning the image in a series of lines
AMRAAM	Advanced Medium-Range Air-to-Air Missile	Escuadron	Squadron (Venezuela)		
		Esk, Eskadrille	Squadron (Danish)	R&D	Research and development
Analogue	Electronic system in which quantities are represented by electrical signals of variable characteristics, i.e. by electrical analogues	EW	Electronic warfare	RNethAF	Royal Netherlands Air Force
		FAéB	Force Aérienne Belge, or Belgian Air Force	RNoAF	Royal Norwegian Air Force
				RWR	Radar-warning receiver
		Fail-operative	System element which will allow a system to continue to operate in its active state in the event of a failure	PRF	Pulse repetition frequency
ANG	Air National Guard			Program	Instructions for a computer
ALR-	US designation for a radar-warning receiver			Programme	Spelling used to designate a programme of research or work
APG-	US designation for a nose-mounted fighter radar	Fail-safe	System element which will revert to a safe condition should it fail		
				Ps	Engineering abbreviation for specific excess power
APQ-	US designation for jamming system	FBW	Fly-by-wire (term for electrically signalled flight-control systems)		
Aspect ratio	Ratio of the span of a wing to its chord			PSP	Programmable signal processor
ASPJ	Advanced Self-Protection Jammer	FLIR	Forward-looking infra-red	SCAMP	Supersonic Cruise Aircraft Modification Programme
ASRAAM	Advanced Short-Range Air-to-Air Missile	g	Unit of acceleration		
Bypass ratio	Ratio of the total airflow through a turbofan engine to that passing through the core section	GAO	General Accounting Office (an investigative branch of the US Congress)	sfc	Specific fuel consumption (unit of fuel consumed per unit of thrust per hour)
		GD	General Dynamics	SFW	Swept-forward wing
		GE	General Electric	smart bomb	Free-falling bomb with built-in guidance system
Camber	Curvature of the centreline of a wing aerofoil	GHz	GigaHertz (Hertz × 1,000,000,000)		
		HUD	Head-up display	Software	One or more programs for a computer
Category 3 flight test	Operational stage of US certification process – now called Air Force Development, Test and Evaluation	Hz	Hertz (unit of frequency)	Synthetic-aperture radar	Technique by which a small radar antenna on a moving vehicle may simulate a larger unit in terms of resolution
		I&A	Integration and assembly		
		IDFAF	Israel Defence Force – Air Force		
CCV	Control-configured vehicle	IIR	Imaging infra-red		
Centre of pressure	Point at which all the lift on the chord of a wing would act if the distributed pressure were to be replaced by a single resultant force	I/J-band	Radar frequencies from 8 to 12GHz	TAC	Tactical Air Command
		IOC	Initial operating capability	Taileron	All-moving tailplane able to move differentially as a substitute for traditional aileron control
		IR	infra-red		
		iron bomb	conventional free-falling high-explosive bomb		
c.g.	Centre of gravity			TFG	Tactical Fighter Group
Chord	Imaginary line connecting the leading and trailing edge of a wing	JTIDS	Joint Tactical Information Distribution System	TFS	Tactical Fighter Squadron
				TFTS	Tactical Fighter Training Squadron
CRT	Cathode-ray tube (computer/TV-style display screen)	KHz	kiloHertz (Hertz × 1,000)	TFW	Tactical Fighter Wing
		KLu	Koninklijke Luchtmacht, or Royal Netherlands Air Force	Trim drag	Component of drag due to the deflection of an elevator or elevon in order to maintain lateral balance of an aircraft
DARPA	Defense Advanced Research Projects Agency				
		kT	Kiloton		
dB	Decibel (unit of gain or attenuation)	Ku-band	Radar frequencies from 12 to 20GHz	TWT	Travelling-wave tube (power source used in many modern radar)
Dead-stick	Flight operation carried out with engine(s) shut down or otherwise inoperative	LANTIRN	Low-Altitude Navigation and Targeting by Infra-Red at Night		
				USAF	United States Air Force
		Mach	Unit equal to the speed of sound	USN	United States Navy
Digital	Electronic system in which quantities are as on/off signals coded to represent numbers	MSIP	Multinational Staged Improvement Programme	Wave drag	Component of drag resulting from the formation of shock waves
		MTU	Maintenance Training Unit		
		MW	Megawatt	Wing loading	Weight of an aircraft divided by the wing area
Drag-at-lift	Drag created under high-lift flight conditions	nav/attack	Navigation and attack (e.g. 'nav/attack system')		
ECM	Electronic countermeasures				

Specification

	YF-16	F-16A	F-16B	F-16C	F-16D
Length	46ft 6in/14.17m	49ft 3.6in/15.03m	49ft 3.6in/15.09m	49ft 3.6in/15.09m	49ft 3.6in/15.09m
Wingspan	30ft 0in/9.14m	31ft 0in/9.45m	31ft 0in/9.45m	31ft 0in/9.45m	31ft 0in/9.45m
Height	16ft 3in/4.95m	16ft 8.5in/5.09m	16ft 8.5in/5.09m	16ft 8.5in/5.09m	16ft 8.5in/5.09m
Weights					
Empty	13,595lb/6,167kg	16,292lb/7,390kg	16,904lb/7,667kg	19,020lb/8,627kg	19,517lb/8,853kg
take-off air-to-air	17,500lb/7,940kg	23,810lb/10,800kg	23,298lb/10,568kg	25,071lb/11,273kg	25,071lb/11,372kg
Maximum take-off	27,000lb/12,247kg	35,400lb/16,057kg	35,400lb/16,060kg	42,300lb/19,184kg	42,300lb/19,184kg
Wing area	300sq ft/27.87sq m	300sq ft/27.87sq m			
Wing loading (air-to-air)		731lb/sq ft/30.81kg/sq m			
Thrust:weight ratio (air-to-air)		1.1:1			
Maximum speed	Mach 2.2	Mach 2+	Mach 2.2+	Mach 2.2+	Mach 2.2+
Service ceiling	>60,000/18,300m	>50,000ft/15,240m	50,000/15,240m	>50,000/15,240m	>50,000/15,240m
Range					
Ferry (with ext. tanks)		>2,100nm/3,890km+	>2,100nm/3,890km+	>2,100nm/3,890km+	>2,100nm/3,890km+
Tactical radius		>800nm/1,480km	>800nm/1,480km	>700nm/1,295km	>700nm/1,295km
Internal fuel		6,972lb/3,162kg			
No. of hardpoints		nine			
Maximum ordnance load	8,800lb/3,990kg	20,450lb/9,280kg	20,450lb/9,280kg+	20,450lb/9,280kg+	20,450lb/9,280kg+

Picture credits

The publishers wish to thank the following organizations who have supplied photographs for this book:

Page 4: both GD. **5:** GD. **6:** top left: Texas Instruments; cedntre: GD. **7:** both GD. **8:** top left: US Department of Defense; top right and bottom: GD. **9:** top left: GD; top right: USAF; bottom; US Department of Defense; **10:** both GD. **11:** Fokker. **12:** Foekker. **13:** SABCA. **14–15:** both GD. **16:** US Department of Defense. **17:** both GD. **18:** top: GD; bottom: Belgian Air Force. **19:** GD. **21:** Belgian Air Force. **22:** US Department of Defense. **23:** centre left: USAF; centre right: GD. **24:** top: USAF; bottom: US Department of defense. **25:** both Pratt & Whitney. **26:** USAF. **27:** top; Pratt & Whitney; bottom: GD. **28:** USAF. **29:** top: Pratt & Whitney; bottom: General Electric. **30:** top: Westinghouse; bottom: Marconi Avionics. **31:** both GD. **33:** top: USAF; bottom: Westinghouse. **34:** both Westinghouse. **35:** top: GD; bottom left and right: Marconi Avionics. **36:** Marconi Avionics. **37:** Top and bottom: US Department of Defense; centre: Westinghouse. **38:** Top: GD; centre left: Lear Siegler; centre right: Netherlands Ministry of Defense. **40:** top; USAF; bottom: GD. **41:** top: GD; centre left: British Aerospace Dynamics; centre right: US Department of Defense; bottom: General Electric. **42:** Hughes Aircraft. **43:** GD. **44:** top left and lower right: GD; top right: Texas Instruments; bottom left: Hughes Aircraft. **45:** top: GD; bottom: Kongsberg Vapenfabrikk. **46:** USAF. **47:** top: GD; bottom: USAF. **48:** both USAF. **49:** top: US Navy; bottom: US Department of Defense. **50:** top: Royal Netherlands Air Force; bottom: Royal Norwegian Air Force. **51:** top: GD; bottom: Royal Danish Air Force. **52:** both GD. **53:** centre: US Department of Defense. **55:** US Department of Defense. **56:** both GD. **57:** top: USAF; bottom: GD. **58–9:** all GD. **60:** top: Vehicle Systems Development Corp; bottom: GD. **61:** both GD. **62:** GD. **63:** top: GD; bottom: US Department of Defense.